THE HAPPY BODY MINDSTYLE

I Got This

The Art of Getting Grit

ALSO BY ANIELA AND JERZY GREGOREK

Non-Fiction
The Happy Body (2009)
The Happy Body Journal (forthcoming)

Poetry
Sacred and Scared (2014)
Food for Your Soul (2014)
Family Tree (forthcoming)
Locket (forthcoming)
No Future, So They Say (forthcoming)

Dialogues
The Happy Body: Mastering Food Choices (2015)
The Happy Body: Mastering Exercise Choices (2015)
The Happy Body: Mastering Rest Choices (2015)

Translations
Late Confession by Józef Baran (1997)
Watermarks by Bogusław Żurakowski (2000)
Her Miniature by Zbigniew Czuchajowski (2000)
In a Flash by Józef Baran (2000)
The Poetry of Maurycy Szymel (2004)
The Shy Hand of a Jew by Maurycy (Mosze) Szymel (2013)
Native Foreigners (2015)

CD
Food for Your Soul (2013)

Videos
The Happy Body Ambience (2013)
The Happy Body Exercise Program (2014)

THE HAPPY BODY MINDSTYLE

I Got This

The Art of Getting Grit

Stories by
Aniela Gregorek

Lectures & Poems by
Jerzy Gregorek

The Happy Body Press
Woodside, California
2016

*To our teachers and mentors who opened the power of words to us
and to our clients who manifested their magic*

CONTENTS

INTRODUCTION

Six years ago when we published our book *The Happy Body*, we considered it a practical manual. Anyone can follow our simple science of nutrition, exercise and relaxation in order to lose weight, reverse serious health conditions and slow the aging process.

The Happy Body is a program based on standards and goals that our clients achieve following our "recipe." It uses step-by-step, easy to follow charts and formulas, along with concise written instructions, detailing a personalized fitness plan consisting of 18 exercises that one can do in their own home with a set of hand weights. The book demonstrates how to do each exercise the right way so as to avoid injuries, and it includes guidelines that enable each person to customize a routine for their body type, fitness and health goals, and progress. We outline how to precisely calculate how much fat one will lose, the muscle gained, what one can expect their body to look like, and exactly how long it will take to reach an ideal body size and shape synchronizing all three elements— nutritional guidelines, exercise program, and relaxation technique.

We found that 20 percent of those who followed the program had great results, drastically transforming their health and fitness, but 80 percent would either make detours, start and stop, or simply loose steam. It puzzled us—how could this twenty percent follow the program and achieve what the rest could not?

We work one-on-one, mentoring individuals to help them to achieve the standards of The Happy Body Program and we actually ask a lot of our clients—we ask them to change. Change doesn't happen easily, and for some it seems impossible. Through patiently educating clients, opening up their imaginations, and coming up with likely scenarios they'll encounter, we give them a new script: the power to decide what to do, and how to do it.

The Happy Body Program asks them to go from an average, repetitive, comforting existence to one where they feel challenged and alive, and suddenly visible. It asks them to take charge of their own lives, make choices and be responsible for them. Not to blame or complain but find solutions within themselves—not only physically but emotionally, as well. That's a lot to ask. We liken this kind of change to going for a Master's degree: the student is not the same when she finishes; she is more knowledgeable, a master in her profession. The only difference is that someone who pursues an advanced degree knows it's not going to be easy and willingly adjusts to the new lifestyle to achieve what she wants: a diploma. She makes that conscious choice.

When it comes to our lifestyle we have a choice in whether or not to exercise, how to eat, and whether or not to make space for relaxation in our life. This is where it starts to be very difficult to make a choice; our preferences, culture, habits, and our emotions will dictate what we are choosing, even though intellectually we know what is good for us.

This book is complementary to our first book *The Happy Body*, which details the foundation of the program, but there is a critical gap between knowing and doing. To bridge that space, we need to change our mind in order to achieve what we want, following The Happy Body plan and strategy. For example, if we think about the dilemma of smoking, most people now know why it's unhealthy. And yet some of us continue to engage in a destructive activity out of habit and for emotional reasons. This is the gap, the pivotal area that *I Got This* addresses, bringing light to the reasons people can fail in the program. We have found that emotional intelligence is the key to achieving success in every area of the program, transforming the "old" mind into one that can support our desire to change.

It is not the rational mind that is making the wrong decision; it is the other side of the mind, the "irrational" side that involves our emotions, memories, attachments, and habits. If this area is ignored, we fail. This book is designed to help build emotional intelligence by offering the right words at the right time for the right person. Everyone's experience is different, so we offer a wide range of stories, lectures and poems to inspire and motivate each person in their pursuit of change. Stories entertain, providing associations where the reader identifies and empathizes with the characters and events that move them and feel compelling. Life lessons provide education for the intellect on one of twelve topics that help the reader understand the how and why of doing the difficult but necessary work. Poems relating to the topic of the lecture offer surprising insights and engage the emotions. We are all emotional beings. Emotions can drive us to do great things or create unwanted consequences, but emotions themselves can never be destroyed, they must be worked with.

All of these elements help to build the Happy Body Mindstyle, the grit that enables real success. We hope that this book will work like a magic elixir in times of weakness, giving you the inner strength to say *I got this.*

CHAPTER 1

The Call

To me, the American Dream is being able to follow your own personal calling. To be able to do what you want to do is incredible freedom.

—Maya Lin

Tourism vs. Immigration

When I ask people whether they like to travel, they always say yes. They love exploring new cultures, tasting new foods, experiencing local customs, architecture, the natural environment and so on. They say that differences from their own culture generate a feeling of newness and excitement.

Then I ask them whether they would want to stay in one of these countries indefinitely. This prompts most people to start to think. They say that although they like to travel, they are always happy to return home. When they are away, they miss what they left behind. Familiarity and predictability are comforting.

What's the difference between going abroad as a tourist vs. for the purpose of immigration? Both journeys will expose you to different environments and lifestyles. But the emotions one experiences as a tourist are quite different from those of a new immigrant who intends to remain at the destination permanently. Immigration naturally involves many anxieties and a certain level of discomfort: learning a new language, finding a job and a place to live, making new friends and so on. Why, then, would people want to go through something so difficult and discomforting?

Because they want to make their lives better, and immigration at least brings opportunity and hope for a better life.

In my case, growing up in Poland, I studied Russian for eight years. I viewed it as the language of Tolstoy and Pushkin: rich, poetic and melodious. It was beautiful to my ears. Jerzy, on the other hand, always disliked Russian, because of its political associations. Russia (and later the Soviet Union) was Poland's oppressor, the cause of Poland's poverty and misery for centuries.

I never imagined that my life would have turned out as it did, especially the act of leaving my native country for an unknown future on the other side of the world.

When Jerzy and I first arrived in the United States, we knew no one. We landed in New York and spent our first day in Detroit, where our sponsor was located, but promptly made our way to California because it was where we wanted to be. With the money we had saved in Sweden and Germany, we purchased our tickets and arrived at LAX.

My Russian wasn't of much use, but Jerzy had studied British English at a academy in Warsaw, so he was able to get into the swing of things immediately, obtaining a driver's license and a job as a personal trainer at a gym in Burbank, bordering Hollywood. After a month, we settled into a small rented cottage close to the gym where Jerzy worked, and a record store (before the days of CDs and DVDs) where I found a job organizing records. At least I was familiar with the alphabet, as both Polish and English are derived from Latin.

Jerzy observed that my English was not improving fast enough, partly because of the nature of my first job, which did not involve much conversation. One day he suddenly announced, "This is the last time I will speak to you in Polish. Starting tomorrow, we will speak only English. This will help us to assimilate and feel that we belong here, in the country we have chosen to be our new home."

At first I thought he couldn't be serious. I could hardly communicate in English! About all I knew how to say was, "My name is Aniela," "I am Polish" and "I can only speak a little English." How could we possibly communicate in English?" I wondered, especially as we were both big talkers.

Well, the next morning all that came out of Jerzy's mouth was English, although I was still speaking to him in Polish. I thought this was ridiculous, as we were both Polish. I became increasingly frustrated when he wouldn't give in. After a few days, when it became apparent that nothing would deter Jerzy from his decision, I reached for a dictionary whenever I wanted to talk. As the days went by, I would use my visits to the grocery store, the local laundromat, and so on to practice the new phrases I had learned.

Then it came time for me to make a decision about my plans for employment. My desire was to work at the gym, coaching. I already had a couple of clients whom I coached at the gym where Jerzy worked. For the most part, I communicated with gestures and body language. To explain well required better English.

My boss at the record store had dangled a raise in front of me as an incentive to continue working there (sales had increased after I got everything in order) but I thanked him and instead enrolled at a local community college during the day, while in the evening I took ESL classes at a high school within walking distance of our cottage. This greatly boosted the speed at which I progressed. I spent a lot of time in the language lab on campus, reading novels (still with the aid of a dictionary but I was having a lot of fun learning).

During our first years in the U.S., we met many immigrants from Poland, as well as other countries. We observed how they had recreated their own little Poland, Italy or Germany. Many of them spoke little or no English. They shopped at their own ethnic grocery stores, consumed the same foods and drinks they were accustomed to, listened to music and sang songs from the old country and went to churches where the services were in their native languages.

Jerzy and I used to make bets when we were in public places as to whether a person was an immigrant, without talking to them or even hearing them speak. What distinguished immigrants from others was their clothes, shoes and hairstyles—even the way they smelled. They were clearly homesick for what was familiar to them, as everything around them was so different and unfamiliar.

There are different ways to approach something new. You either plunge into it or you try to do it gradually, which can actually be more difficult, living in-between. Jerzy's decision to speak with me only in English was one of the best things that had ever happened to me, even though at the time it was difficult and frustrating. I began to appreciate his decision after I had developed a certain distance from the changeover, from the perspective of the question, "What if we hadn't done that? What would my life be like now?"

Years later we heard the story of general Cortés. In 1519, the Aztec Empire covered about 80,000 miles in central and southern Mexico and was inhabited by almost 6 million people, when Spanish Conquistador Hernando Cortés arrived with 508 soldiers, 100 sailors and 16 horses to begin his conquest. After his men came ashore, Cortés ordered them to burn the ships. He wanted his men to be in the state of mind to either win or die. By 1521, Cortés and his small army had conquered the Aztecs. We know that superior weaponry helped the Spanish but also we know that Cortés' strategy and his commitment to it was also necessary to win the war.

Jerzy's intuitive approach to "burn the ships"—in our case stop using Polish at home—sped up our process of adjusting and assimilating to our life in the States.

Why am I telling you this story? What does all of this have in common with The Happy Body, or life?

A lot, actually, because The Happy Body is a lifestyle and it requires change. You will find yourself going through a similar process of change as you would if you were to immigrate to a different country. New habits must be developed in order for you to make the transition. You will need to change your language to one of empowerment, replacing "hope" or "wish" with "will." To achieve and stand behind what you want, look for solutions within, understand the why and how and how much, because in the end it is your life that you shape and own.

No doubt you have "visited" many fitness programs, maybe tested some approaches, and even enjoyed your visits, but nothing really worked to your satisfaction. You certainly were not persuaded to change your status from tourist to immigrant. If you explored yoga, for example, you got more flexible but there was no nutritional guidance. So if you had wanted to lose fat, you would have had to look for some other program to complement that. If you wanted to get stronger, you lifted weights, but you still would have had to stretch in order to become more flexible. And so on and so forth. This kind of approach only creates a lot of frustration because it doesn't establish a holistic approach to health and fitness.

We present The Happy Body to you as a complete, integrated and effective program, a lifestyle — and a destination worthy of immigrating to, after an initial visit.

Triple Happiness

As a child, I believed that everyone was born with the same potential for happiness and that everything depended on our choices, passion and hard work. This romantic notion was crushed when I learned that even at birth, at the very beginning of our journey, some people were not as fortunate as others. It is true that most of us are born to decent parents with good intentions. For many of us, however, happiness is chipped away at the very moment of birth—or even before that. Unfortunately, some of us are born into families of hate, flooded by various parental addictions, and lacking in certain resources, often those as basic as heat and food. When we are hungry or in a condition of discomfort, we cry. Some of us are immediately fed and comforted. Others are not.

When we begin walking, our world becomes bigger and there are many more reasons to be happy or unhappy. When we reach for a toy that is not ours, those of us who are lucky are told, "Do you like that toy? I can buy that for you." Those of us who are not so lucky are told, "Don't touch it. It's not yours," after which the toy is pulled forcefully from our hands. After the experience is repeated frequently enough, we learn to adapt.

As toddlers, the world expands and so do the reasons for crying about something: siblings and playmates who are stronger, who push us and take things away from us we don't want them to take. If what was taken was ours, we can usually get it back by telling our mothers about what happened. But if it was not ours, we usually don't get it back, no matter how hard we cry. At this time, we are taught the rule of possession and being nice if we want something that does not belong to us. This can sometimes help us get what we want.

When we go to kindergarten, our world is even bigger. There are things in the kindergarten classroom that don't belong to any individual student. We learn about sharing, in spite of our natural instincts.

As we grow up, we still have pressing desires, sometimes needing and wanting things but not always getting what we want. Of course, we all learn how to deal with jealousy by pretending that we do not want what others are getting. From that time on, even when somebody has something that we would like to have but cannot get, we express a lack of interest in it. In this way, we tell the richer that we cannot be controlled.

As we enter our teens, differences become even more visible. Almost everything is controlled by money: where we live, the school we attend, the restaurants where we dine, the seats where we sit on a plane. It becomes obvious that we need to distinguish ourselves in some way. We need something within everyone's reach that is not controlled by money.

This is when some discover sports. Of course, not all sports are accessible to people without money, like golf, for example, or sailing. But most sports are available to everyone: basketball, soccer or track and field. We have fun for a while until we learn that if we are too short, our chances of excelling are slim. Almost no one succeeds in basketball who is less than six feet tall—and statistically most men are shorter than that.

At this point, you may be thinking, "Jerzy is crazy. It doesn't matter whether somebody is tall or short. We are all born equal and have the same chances of success in life." Well, I almost believed in that, too—especially after I graduated from college, when I won many world weightlifting championships, and created The Happy Body Program. But one day when I was waiting for my daughter at her school, I talked to a mother who was standing with her two daughters, waiting for the third. Suddenly a friend of the woman joined us and said to one of the daughters, "Oh, my god, you're so tall!" The girl beamed. After the girl's smile faded, the woman turned to the other daughter, who had grown little over the past year, and said nothing. The girl turned her head away and stared ahead, tightening her lips. Even the tall girl looked away.

Smiling, the woman said to the mother, "I haven't seen you in ages."

The mother responded with the same beaming smile, "It has been a long time. Let's plan on getting together more often." At this point, I saw my daughter and it was time to go.

As I was driving home, the woman's words echoed in my mind: "You are so tall." Finally, I flipped the meaning, thinking to myself: "You are so short." I immediately understood the comparison. Saying "You are so short" would be offensive, which is why people don't say it. Society imposes the judgment on all of us that being short is not as good as being tall. Then I thought about other comparisons that prove that at the time of birth, we are already more or less fortunate. We might say, "You look so beautiful." We would never say, "You look so ugly." We would say, "You are so smart." We would not say, "You are so stupid." We might say, "You look so young." We would not say to someone's face, "You look so old."

Those who are not on the receiving end of compliments are fortunate if they discover what can be their best friend: the "even playing field" of the arts. Of course, some money is always needed for paints or renting a piano. But almost everyone can afford a used guitar or at least a pencil and paper to write a story or a poem. We can excel at playing an instrument, singing or writing. And even if we don't have a college degree or a high-paying job, we can exercise some form of artistic expression, one that helps us share with others and derive enjoyment over the years, without suffering from a constant awareness of having been born ugly, poor, short or into a dysfunctional family.

At the same time, we learn that happiness can be very fickle. It comes to us the instant we get things and leaves as we adapt to their presence. We are not happy when we don't have things and not happy when we have them for too long. The constant pursuit of creating something new, something better, is necessary for happiness. That pursuit keeps us youthful and engaged, which in turn makes us satisfied. We need to have a feeling on a daily basis that whatever we do will make our life better.

This approach is more necessary as we age. As we get older and weaker, we need to engage in pursuits that make us better over time. We also need to appreciate what we already have. Aging is a very powerful and destructive force, one that eventually kills us. As such, it is certainly one of the major reasons for our unhappiness. I cannot think of anything other than grace to help us make it along this destructive journey, to make it happy and meaningful.

If you are older than 35, you are already a boat sailing upstream, so don't count on the waters always being smooth and peaceful. They can become aggressive and violent at any time. You will then need a better boat. Don't wait until you get cancer. Rather, do everything you can so as not to contract cancer in the first place. Don't wait until your posture deteriorates so badly that your body is so bent that you can't see ahead anymore and you have to sit in a wheelchair. Make sure that your posture is perfect. Don't wait until you no longer have friends; reach out to people and spend time with them. Enjoy making them laugh and helping them when they need it. Always be at least one step ahead of what could make you unhappy. If you live this way, not only will you be setting an example for your family and friends but for others who may not even know you personally. You'll be so engaged with life that you won't even know when you reach a hundred.

To progress over time and become better at doing things, we develop a mind that is able to do what is difficult yet good for us, even though we don't like it. As we keep practicing what is good for us, occasionally we feel joy while doing it and the better we are, the more joy we have. When we reach mastery, the moments of happiness outweigh the moments of dissatisfaction and we begin a life of a constant joy.

Achieving results takes practice and time, however. In the case of education, some students are unable to get into college or to progress once they gain entry. They are unable to practice enough or adapt to the new demands and either drop off or are expelled.

At that point we need to catch up and progress faster to do what others can do who are already ahead of us. Usually we undertake tasks that require more time than we think, and because of this we either hurt ourselves or burn out and stop. We desire a quick fix and instead of increasing our knowledge we believe that we can get better by outsmarting the system. But knowledge is like learning the piano—there are small daily increments that must happen before we progress. For the first time we are aware that time divides us; to play like others who are on a higher level we need to practice a certain amount of time—and that can be years. But we cannot wait to be happy until we achieve all our goals, so we need to learn how to be happy while working on improving our skills. Satisfaction lies in the process: Enjoying every movement while repeating the same gymnastic routine over and over or preparing breakfast every day for our children before they leave for school.

You Are Asking

Mom, why don't you complain?
It is not my time.
When I asked your grandma
the same question, she told me,
It's okay that sometimes
you don't do your homework
because you want to play,
but it wouldn't be right for me
to forget about cooking dinner.
Of course, sometimes it's hard
but I do it happily anyway
because I know
you will remember my face.
Do you really think that life
without complaining is possible?
You are asking, aren't you?

Imagine you have a conversation with another version
of yourself that you write as a dialogue:
"I've searched for happiness for a long time and I see
that you're always happy. How do you do it?"
"I thought of sharing the secret with you after I found
it, but after many years I gave up trying to reach you."
"It took me many years to ask you because I am proud,
I was too ashamed, but today I'm ready. Please tell me
how you can be so happy all the time, even in the evening
when you're tired?"

"Well, I don't know what your definition of 'happiness' is. Can you tell me?"

"What would be the best way to tell you? It's the best feeling that you can have."

"Can you be more specific?"

"Sometimes I watch you when you write a letter or when you sit with tea before going to bed. You have this glow of satisfaction that I identify as happiness."

"So if I understand you, you name the feeling I have when I write or I enjoy a cup of tea at the end of the day."

"That's right."

"Then let me tell you my secret. Every morning before showering I sit quietly in a chair for ten minutes and I contemplate what I will do during the day. Then I write it out and after breakfast I go and make it happen. As I make each goal happen I feel a sense of accomplishment and it makes me feel good. When I write a good sentence I smile to myself and when I sit with a cup of tea before going to bed I contemplate all the things I planned and achieved during the day. As I remember what I planned and what I achieved I am very content and feel good. This is what I think people identify as happiness."

"It seems to me that you experience double happiness. You are happy when doing what you planned and you are happy accomplishing it."

"Right."

"Then let me ask you this: Do you need to know the word happiness or even be aware of it to actually experience it?"

"Actually you are the proof of this."

"I must say that you did not tell me what happiness is and how to get it, but you told me how to experience it. So I must thank you for the great lesson. Now I know how to become happiness and how not to chase it. From today on I will give a hundred percent of my focus to the things I do, so I will enjoy the process. And when I make progress I will appreciate it and feel good."

When you start The Happy Body, focus on what you will be doing and give it all of your attention. As a result, you will forget about the world around you, and you will let your whole body resonate with whatever you're doing. When you learn the exercises, slow down the movement to the smallest detail. The Happy Body exercises will give you an opportunity to experience mindfulness and a meditative way of training. The steps in every exercise are singular, so the brain focuses completely on what the body is doing. Become inhale, tighten, lift, stretch, return, and exhale every time when you do it. Exercising like this, your mind will stop wandering and your body will resonate with the movement. Happiness will flood your body and you will get stronger and more flexible without even noticing it. And when you comprehend the results, a powerful appreciation will vibrate within every cell of your being. From now on, when you open any door to any room you will walk through it like a master—loving yourself and everyone you see. In this way you have achieved triple happiness. First, you're happy because of the results: you're more youthful and stronger.

Second, you're happy because you're the one who achieved your goal; you're proud of staying on course. And third, this happiness radiates out to others, increasing the joy around you.

BETWEEN

I cannot survive on
thirteen hundred calories.
It's starvation.
What if it is enough?
his nutritionist asked.
I don't care. I want to eat more.
Then you need to write a letter to the man upstairs,
said the nutritionist, pointing his finger to the sky.
To God?
Yes. I don't know anyone else who can
allow you to eat more food
than you need and not get fat.
I still don't like it. There must be another way.
There is.
What is it?
You need to write a letter to the one downstairs.
I don't like that, either. Any other way?
Yes.
No letter.

CHAPTER 2

Awakening

That is the real spiritual awakening, when something emerges from within you that is deeper than who you thought you were. So, the person is still there, but one could almost say that something more powerful shines through the person.

—Eckhart Tolle

Dream On but Act Now

From time to time, we all have moments when we pause to think, to feel, to reevaluate our lives. This might happen on New Year's Eve or out of the blue, say, when you meet a friend from high school. Looking at her and listening to her bubbling over lunch, it seems she is so happy with her life. Her job is interesting and well paid, the house she lives in is impressive, her boyfriend (a CEO) is handsome and in love with her. But as for you....

You feel your life sucks. Your job was supposed to be only temporary, to pay your bills for a while, until the right time comes to do the kind of meaningful work that matters to you. In addition to that, your boss is a nightmare and the pay is low. And that is not all: you live in a crappy apartment building with the smell of frying onions and cat's pee lingering in the hallways. Your husband is a jerk and he doesn't understand you.

Then what do you do after the meeting? You start dreaming: If only I moved to sunny Italy and had a husband who was not a locksmith but a lawyer. Then life would be so wonderful.

You go home and you start barking at your husband and kids, you grumble about the rainy weather and the price of gas. In the kitchen, you slam pots and pans and that becomes the evening music that goes along with your cooking.

The only bearable moments come after everyone else has gone to bed. You then nestle into your worn-out couch, to watch a romantic movie or read a novel about someone who turned her life around. Just like emotional eating, movies become the most immediate escape from our own reality, feeding our longing for what could be, if only ....

If it's true that ten percent of life is what happens to us and the other ninety percent is how we respond, then why do we look for a solution outside of us, rather than within?

Over and over again, we fall for this magic thing. Inspiration, motivation ... Oh yes, the willing to suspend disbelief when we watch a movie. But what is the message for our children in movies like "Nanny McPhee," which by the way I really enjoyed, except ... It made me think about us, as parents: What do we do when children who are out of control need to be disciplined? Most movies contain an element of magic or the supernatural, which leaves us with some kind of feeling, but not much of a solution about what we can do to help ourselves. We viewers look for inspiration, motivation, something to move us. We might be moved emotionally but most of the time, that is where we stop. We are still waiting for a superman or a hero to appear to help or rescue us. And we dream of having supernatural powers like Nanny McPhee or at least dream of getting a nanny like that. What we get, usually, is a nanny from hell who needs to be taught how to drive and cook and even how to change a diaper. And oftentimes we'll need to take care of her, as well, when she's not able to make a car payment. And that's life. Our life.

So we dream of changing our lives, our jobs, where we live, the people with whom we share our lives, losing weight. And the list goes on and on. We watch others changing their lives, but you, well, you make up a list of "if onlys" ....

When I visited Poland in 1990, after the fall of the Berlin Wall, I had an interesting conversation with my teenage niece. At sixteen, she talked to me about what she felt was wrong with her life. She then elaborated on how wonderful America was, along with the lifestyle of the people living there. She knew all of this, of course, from magazines, movies and TV. She raved about how fun, creative, easy—in one word, fantastic—life would be for her, if she only lived 'there' and not 'here.'

Many of us dream of changing our lives but the list of "if onlys" adds up, so we never change or even try to start unlocking our unhappy, unfulfilled lives. We base our failings on the places where we live, the people we share our lives with, the weather and so on.

Where do we start? How do we turn our situations around? Radical changes rarely work and we risk losing whatever cumulative gains we have made so far. So maybe it's wise to look at yourself and your life and find a solution that is not a quick fix. That would be a steady, progressive approach to changing from within, leading to tangible results. The best way to start would be by identifying an affordable approach that would enable you to achieve the desired changes wherever you are— whether living in an old apartment, with your husband of fifteen years, holding whatever job you currently have— to create a life that would bring you joy and fulfillment.

I asked my niece if we could explore her situation a bit. What if she were to look at the place she lived in and her life from a different perspective? And so we did. One major complaint she had was boredom and lack of money. Could she do things that don't require much or any money, to entertain and educate herself? I asked her about the history of the town she lived in and the neighboring ones. What about all the interesting people like writers, painters, athletes and musicians who lived in the place she called her hometown? How engaged was she in her own surroundings?

Engagement would mean going to museums, visiting the local library and local art exhibitions. How often did she go to see performances at local theatres? Did she participate in the local community center? Did she go swimming in winter in the public swimming pool? How often did she go to the nearby lake, for a half-day retreat? How about initiating some activity that you are passionate about, I asked her, and starting a new group where everyone would have fun, cooking or making crafts or discussing books? The list of ideas could go on, and we did make a long list of fun, creative and educational things to do.

Well, we discovered that she didn't need to move to New York or to Paris and live in an apartment overlooking the Eiffel Tower to awaken the artist within. Novels are fun to read but most of them are to be found in the section of the bookstore labeled "Fiction."

At the end of our conversation, I suggested that she become her own hero (or heroine, to be more exact), not falling for stories like Under the Tuscan Sun or Eat, Pray, Love. These books are written primarily to entertain. Maybe some are intended to inspire people to reach for what they want in life, modeling how to live life to the fullest. But in any event, these pages are a product where the author was paid for writing her experience and it was her job. These stories hardly ever resemble the real life of an ordinary person. I suggested that she write her own story.

We live in a time of abundance and it is easy to be distracted or diverted from what we really want. We are bombarded by information and images of what other people want us to think, feel or do. Today the public obsesses the most about three major categories: food, exercise and relaxation.

Many of us are seduced into buying things with a promise that our life will change for the better. Only if we get the newest "thigh master" or eat low-calorie cookies can we lose weight. Only if we could go on a vacation to a faraway place can we relax and eliminate our stress. Years ago I saw an advertisement showing a family preparing to go on a road trip. There was a lot of commotion in the house with parents and children running around frantically, packing their bags. They left behind a big mess in the house to which they would of course return. Finally, they got into the car loaded with things, with little room for themselves. After traveling, I imagined for hours, they arrived in a hotel room, exhausted. They brought all their stuff into the room and collapsed in front of the TV. They were all gaping at the flashing screen, with blank expressions on their faces.

A false notion of "necessities" prompts us to fail in all three areas (food, exercise and relaxation) because we don't know how much is enough. The result is that abundance leads to waste. We overdo it with things that offer temporary improvements, make us feel better temporarily (like manicures, facial treatments and massages), at the expense of things that offer more long-term value (like knowledge or skills that we acquire or cultivate). The latter would apply to pursuits such as painting, playing a musical instrument or practicing The Happy Body Program.

My advice to my niece was not to obsess about food, exercise or stress but rather to follow THB Program. THB Program is like a sport. Its purpose is to improve peoples' lives, making them simpler and more purposeful. It is meant to provide an appropriate perspective on food and exercise, which is necessary for staying healthy and fit in our modern-day world. After achieving the standards of THB, many of our clients turn their attention to pursuing some form of art or craft, such as painting, pottery making, cooking or writing. Whatever it happens to be, this new pursuit enhances their lives, creating a new sense of excitement and adventure. They participate in a community that is creative and purposeful. Since they are passionate about what they do, a common bond develops between them. They have fun on their journey toward getting better at what they do.

Now is the time for you to become your own hero or heroine. Become your own celebrity. Dream on but act now.

Aging

If you could hear life talking to you when you were born, it might say something like this: "Welcome, my lovely child, into this wonderful world. Until you reach the age of 18, I will make you taller, stronger and more beautiful with each passing year." If you are at least 18, you know that life has kept its promise. You got taller and stronger whether you liked it or not. And of course everyone at 18 is beautiful. If it happens that you are a woman who is 5' 8," you became strong enough to lift 75 pounds above your head. If you are a man you who grew to be 6 feet tall, you became strong enough to lift 150 pounds.

It is nothing but happiness and joy at that age. If you could hear life talking, it might say: "You are already strong and ready to bear fruit. Nothing will change for you for the next 18 years. Enjoy being powerful and creative. When I talk to you the next time, you will probably have a wife and children and will have worked hard for many years to help your children have everything they need to grow as tall and strong as you have." Time passes by very quickly between the ages of 18 and 36.

If you could hear life speaking to you when you are 36, it might say this: "I made you strong and tall and kept you that way for all these years but now it is time for some changes. Of course I do not want anything too drastic because you still have major responsibilities. You will eventually become a grandparent. You will need to help your children by helping care for your grandchildren sometimes. From this point on, you will get two percent weaker every year. After another 36 years, you will be preparing for your final goodbyes."

You have nothing much to say, so you surrender to the plan. You wait until things happen to you, the same way they do for everyone else.

But is this true for everyone? You know it isn't necessarily true for athletes. If you become an athlete, through specific training routines, you become stronger than you would be without that training. You can lift 200 or 300 pounds.

When I was 13 years old, I was 5' 5" and I could lift 80 pounds, while many boys were almost six feet tall and could lift more than 100 pounds. My life in the seventh and eighth grades became miserable. Taller and stronger boys challenged me, pulling me into many fights. I knew that I had to get stronger. So I decided to join the weightlifting team and practice diligently every day.

A year later, when I was 14, I could lift 150 pounds. As a result, I gained some respect from taller and stronger boys but fights were still wearing me out. At age 15, I lifted 200 pounds at a local competition. The news spread quickly and from that day on, there was no boy in the school that wanted to fight me. On the contrary, many tall and strong boys wanted to become my friends. Life became easier and more pleasant for me.

At 23, I lifted 330 pounds and nothing changed for a long time. At 36, however, I got a message from life that the time had come for things to start getting worse. Today, at 60, I can lift 220 pounds. During the last 24 years, I lost 110 pounds from my top lift. Every year, I get weaker by 4.5 pounds.

At this rate, it will take another 24 years to lose another 110 pounds. At that time, I will be 84 and as strong as any 18 year old without any weightlifting training. It will take another 24 years after that before I become weak enough to say my final goodbyes. At that time, I will be 108, which seems about right to me. Like anyone who says goodbye after the hundred-year mark, it will probably not happen in a hospital while attached to many tubes, but rather at home in my sleep, while dreaming about the next exciting day to come.

It is true that we all have a clock in our bodies that starts when we are 36 and begins making us weaker every year. All athletes who compete with numbers prove it. Track and field athletes, swimmers, weightlifters and others: like clockwork, they end their careers around the age of 35.

To be fair, athletic competitions are divided into categories by age. From age 12 until 17, girls and boys compete in new categories every two years: 12-13, 14-15 and 16-17. Before athletes are 18, they compete in the Junior Olympics. From 18-35, they compete in the Senior Olympics. After the age of 35, they compete in the Masters Olympics. Senior athletes (18-35) are at their physical peak; different ages can compete in a wider pool because aging has not yet set in for them. A 36-year-old can beat an 18-year-old, just as an 18-year-old can defeat a 36-year-old.

Master division categories are structured on the basis of five-year intervals, so there is a 35-39 division, a 40-44 division and so on. Even though there isn't much difference in terms of years between the age of 35 and the age of 39, athletes who compete definitely feel the difference. As a general rule, it's always easier for a

35-year-old to beat a 39-year-old, simply because of the inevitable process of aging.

Even though it is true that life begins to age us beginning at 36, a person's individual condition at that age is not predetermined. A person may be very weak and have difficulty lifting 50 pounds at that age. Or he could be very strong, capable of lifting 300 pounds. The process of aging in these two scenarios is quite different. It will take a considerably longer time for the stronger individual to lose strength to the point of being unable to carry his own groceries. For the weaker one, however, that process might only take a few years.

So if you realize that aging begins at 36 but the specifics of the process are not predetermined, you can alter the way you age. Even if you happen to already be 60, you can still improve considerably because there is a lot of reserve power that you have previously not been aware of, but are now. If, for example, you are now 60 and can only lift 60 pounds, while a world champion at the same age can lift 220 pounds, this means that you have 180 pounds in reserve. We know that you will become weaker by two percent each year. But if you improve by four percent each year, you will actually experience a net improvement of two percent. So instead of lifting 58.2 pounds, you will lift 61.2 pounds. The same is true for anyone else. Aging starts for everyone at the same time but the specifics relating to condition and quality are within our control.

A year ago, I tried to explain the importance of getting stronger to a 60-year-old friend who happens to be a Zen master. I told him that I had an indestructible body. He laughed and told me that every body is destructible. I told him that if my body can lift 200 pounds and whatever I need to do in life only requires at most the lifting of 40 pounds, then it is almost impossible to hurt my body because I am only using 20 percent of its strength.

He thought for a moment and said, "I got it. You are like a boat traveling up the river at 40 miles per hour. The down current is moving at a rate of 20 miles per hour. That means that you are actually moving at the rate of 20 miles per hour, without exerting yourself. I, on the other hand, can only lift 40 pounds. So if I want to go up the river at the same speed as you, I would have to use 100 percent of all my strength, the entire time, which means that I could break down at any moment. But since you use only 20 percent, you will never break."

"Exactly," I said. Mark then looked at me and said, "Well, it is obviously time for me to get stronger. I do not want to break at any moment."

When I met Mark a year later, he asked, "How is your boat speed? Mine has improved tremendously. I can now travel up the river at 80 miles per hour."

"That's fantastic," I said. "Congratulations!"

"It wasn't easy. I got a weightlifting coach but after two months, I didn't get any stronger. I just got sore. So I fired him and found another one. The second coach knew right away what to do with me. After only a month, I could lift 60 pounds. After four months, I could lift 70 pounds. After the ten-month point, I lifted 80 pounds, a new personal record. I hadn't understood the need for strength when you first told me about it but the vision of a boat struggling to climb upstream was in my thoughts both day and night.

"The second coach not only helped me lift more weight. He also passed along some valuable wisdom to me. After I lifted 80 pounds, he said, 'OK, Mark. You have invested about ten thousand on your training with me. During this time, you have doubled your strength. If I were to give you twice the amount you paid, on the condition that you dial back your strength to the level it was when you started with me, would you take the money?'

"For a moment, I was speechless. I hadn't been thinking in terms that what I had been getting was priceless. So I said, 'Thank you for helping me realize what money can't buy.'"

Mark paused for a moment and then added, "Actually, if you hadn't helped me realize when aging begins and what I could do to help myself, I would never have taken the action I did to achieve the wonderful results I just told you about. In addition to my trainer, I have you to thank, as well. Today, I'm not only twice as strong as I was when you helped me see the light a year ago. It would now take ten years of aging for my condition to revert to what it was a year ago. Of course, I don't plan to allow that to happen. I plan to get even stronger."

If you are older than 35, being smart does not help anymore. It is time to become wiser than ever. Whatever you did before to stay in shape will no longer work. Andrea had taught aerobics since she was a teen until the age of 40. "Until I was 40 everything worked," she said, "whenever I noticed that I was getting fatter, I would increase my daily aerobic exercise load. The fat was melting away and the pounds were disappearing, but then nothing that I had used before worked. Whenever I tried to increase my exercise I would get hurt or too sore so I had to stop until I recovered. But then I kept getting fatter. It seemed there was no solution to stay fit and that I had to surrender to the process of aging." What Andrea didn't understand is that by doing the wrong exercise she was wearing herself out and that the body could no longer recover. As soon as she learned to use exercise properly and use food to balance her weight, she became lean again.

Aging is inevitable but how we age and how fast it happens depends on our way of living. You can be 70 and stooped over, waiting for a wheelchair or you can be 100 and standing like a tower, excited about a new day coming. The lifestyle of a 100 year old is not much different from a 70-year-old one. Both men have families, children, and grandchildren. They both work and retire. So why not devote 30 minutes a day to something that will keep us healthy and fit until we are 100?

I WILL DRAG MY ASS DOWN

Why don't you exercise?
the trainer asked her client,
a psychologist.
I don't have time.
Listen,
I've used everything I know
to help you change your mind,
but you are stronger than I am.
When this happens,
I send my clients
to a psychologist,
but you are one, so
where should I send you?
The psychologist stared at his trainer,
looking for a way out,
but she did not blink.
Okay, he said,
I will drag my ass down to the gym.

CHAPTER 3

Vision

In order to carry a positive action we must develop here a positive vision.

—Dalai Lama

Why Are We Poor?

Because we're stupid. Why are we stupid? Because we are poor. That's how my mother used to answer my question about why our family was poor. Or, as a matter of fact, any poor family that lived in our neighborhood. It was a vicious cycle, in other words, and the only way to break it was to become wiser. And she was right, because the definition of stupid is not being able to apply what one has learned, for future benefit. Are you poor because you are stupid or is it the other way around? Whatever the order is, if you want to change the situation, you need to start somewhere. That's where an efficient lifestyle plays an important role.

From an early age, I was aware of differences between my family's lifestyle and that of other families. My parents worked hard all their lives. I had never seen them take vacations.

They made mistakes. They made poor decisions. They had poor habits. This all took its toll, reflected in their prematurely aged faces, their hardened bodies and thinning, gray hair. We were one of the poorest families in the neighborhood. I always considered my parents to be good people. Still, they ended up struggling almost all their lives. As children, we watched them wither away, experiencing few moments of happiness. These were the rare times when we were gathered around the table, eating, when food was atypically abundant.

One day while visiting Jerzy's parents, we ran into one of his neighbors, a very pleasant woman in her early 30s. After a short chat, we parted company. As we walked away, Jerzy told me the story about this woman and her family. I still remember that story vividly because it was about the exemplary lifestyle that raised people above their environment, above their poverty, in spite of their life circumstances.

They lived in the same apartment complex as Jerzy's family. The parents had three daughters, all of them a few years older than Jerzy. They were different from all the other neighboring families and people liked to gossip about them. The family lived quietly, in a way that was almost unnoticeable. On Sundays, people would see them walking to the local church or working in their garden, not far from the apartment. Their dress was always simple but neat. Many times, as a child, Jerzy overheard neighbors gossiping about this family. Mostly it was either about the food that they were buying or the clothes they wore: the same dresses or shirts or pants, mended again and again, over time. Although both parents worked, they lived below their means. They would buy only the most basic produce at the local store, eating fruits and vegetables from their own garden. In spite of all the gossip, they looked healthy and slim. But the judgment of some was that this family was excessively thrifty, to the point of being stingy, needlessly depriving their children of things like butter for their bread. They could have led comfortable lives, but they chose foolishly not to do so. "What are they saving the money for," people asked, "to take it to their graves?"

The years passed by and the children in the neighborhood gradually grew up. One day, the news spread that one of the daughters had become a medical doctor.

A couple of years later, the same news spread about the second daughter. Then later, the third. All three girls had become doctors. All of this, while everyone else had been busy living their own lives, in their own way.

Most of the children in the neighborhood were obliged to go to work relatively early in life, taking on menial, low-paying jobs. This was sometimes prompted by the family's financial situation and sometimes due to a lack of drive to continue their educations. It was only occasionally that someone would get a high school diploma.

This family with three daughters who had become physicians repeatedly stirred up feelings of jealousy among the neighbors. It was difficult to observe the frustrations of people who criticized this family just to rationalize their poor choices and failings. These parents were convinced that their own children were just as good and equally intelligent, which was often indeed true.

Being poor to the point where all your thoughts are focused on meeting basic needs takes a lot of energy out of people. Under these conditions, people tend to lose sight of larger and more long-term goals. Feelings of deprivation prompt people to obsess about food, as was the case for my family and other families in our neighborhood.

The members of both Jerzy's family and mine were preoccupied with survival, afraid to think about planning further than a month into the future. That's how we lived: from month to month, from my father's salary that he received at the beginning of the month, to the end of the month. As that was not enough, my mother was sometimes obliged to borrow money from neighbors or do occasional work, such as digging for potatoes or picking mushrooms or blueberries in a nearby forest, with us at her side.

Was it physical poverty or the poverty of the mind that could not change our neighborhood? The family of the three daughters was actually a good role model for those who genuinely wanted to change. This family was gracefully demonstrating how actions in the present were connected with future outcomes. The girls' parents somehow understood that the true purpose of food is to provide nourishment for the body. They also understood another type of nourishment—for the mind and soul—that we often forget, lending a sense of purpose and meaning to life.

Though it seemed to others that the parents had to sacrifice a lot for the future of their children, this wasn't really true. They just deliberately led their lives without overindulgence. I imagined these parents watching their children as adults enjoying meaningful careers. Ultimately, they were all happy, healthy and fairly wealthy.

They were graceful, humble and hard working. They understood what was required to rise above poverty, a combination of attention to lifestyle and emphasis on education. They had a plan and they followed through with it, faithfully and consistently.

It is by making choices that we create our lives. Is it important to first know what you want and then to steadfastly pursue those goals, regardless of what others think or what they do to try to influence you. There will always be someone trying to sell you something. There will always be something you may like to buy, regardless of whether you really need it. Is life about consuming or more about creating and becoming the best you can be? Later on, I came to understand that there are many things over which we in fact have control. Education is one example. Through education, you can better yourself and become the kind of person you want to be.

For some, the experience of life might feel like being on a treadmill: we are born, we grow up, we go to school, we go to work, we get married and so on. There are predictable events that we more or less all go through eventually. It is what we do with the time in between that is important. We should live life in the best way possible, so we feel fulfilled when it's time to go.

From the perspective of time, I see how aging and poverty seem to work in parallel. Quality of life usually worsens both with aging or being poor. Both can be a source of depression. Aging, like poverty, grows on us and if we don't do something about it to slow it down, it gets worse. The older we are, the fewer mistakes we are allowed to make. Otherwise, the consequences can be devastating.

When we are mentally healthy, we have the internal need to survive. We do everything to keep ourselves alive. This includes eating, exercise, rest and emotional fulfillment. When I was a teenager, I once read a book about the lives of factory workers in 19th century England. One of the passages contained an internal monologue, expressing the thoughts of a woman who was exhausted from overwork, underfed, with no prospects for a brighter future, with only one desire on her mind: to die. She prayed for death as one would for liberation. When I read this, it shook me up tremendously because I believe that life is a precious gift. To experience this world is a privilege.

I drive my daughter four times a week to gymnastics practice, so we spend a lot of time together in the car. Driving can be stressful or boring but we make it more fun by listening to audio books, which makes the time pass by quickly. Last week, we both enjoyed listening to Gary Paulsen's Brian's Survival. After we had finished listening, I went to the library to check out other audiobooks by the same author. The librarian Alice, a very friendly woman, asked what I liked about the story because all his books are about survival. I told her what I liked: the concise language, the imagery, the subtlety of descriptions of both internal and external states, enabling the reader to imagine as well as feel. As I talked to her, I realized why I like Gary Paulsen's writing so much. I identify myself as someone who has experienced poverty and extreme circumstances many times in my life. I am also aging and I don't want to feel vulnerable about my future.

We all need a survival kit to ensure our well-being. That means predicting, imagining, planning and so on. For most of us, it's not easy to do that because we just react to what happens to us. Or we give up even before we put any effort into pursuing change.

There is a time in youth when your entire future is ahead of you, making all things seem possible. When you are young and also wise, your life will be lived on purpose and you will feel fulfilled. But the question is, how to be both young and wise? What we lack the most is education, not necessarily of a formal nature.

With sufficient education comes imagination and an appreciation of how our actions will affect our future.

A Goal

Goals serve as a motivation for creating a plan, which involves a strategy for achieving one's dreams. Goals inspire and motivate us, from moment to moment, day to day and year to year, until we arrive at the desired destination.

When I was 13, I was weak in comparison to the stronger boys on the street. Because of this, I was badly bullied and frequently shaken down for money. I decided to put a stop to this; I would gain respect by becoming stronger than any of the other boys. I had a goal but I needed a plan. I knew that it would be impossible for me to develop the strength I wanted seeking guidance from the same people who were bullying me. Instead, I joined the weightlifting team, which was based in a different city, 25 miles away from where I lived. This meant a one-hour train ride each way, but that didn't bother me because my desire to achieve my goal was so much stronger than the effort required to make the trip. I was willing to do anything to get the boys who were bothering me to leave me alone.

At the beginning of my team practice sessions, my coach focused on flexibility. Later, the emphasis was on skills. Finally, the focus was on power. Gradually, I was getting stronger. Without really noticing it, I was being left alone at school, no longer being bullied or shaken down. I walked with my weightlifting friends for hours through the streets of our town every day, talking about weightlifting: all the different strategies, plans, tactics, other weightlifters, competitions and so on. We had girlfriends, we enjoyed going to parties together and playing volleyball, but mostly we just talked about weightlifting.

Ten years later, I was working in a fire department and preparing myself for college. One day, I was passing by the cluster of apartment buildings where we lived. About a hundred boys were lifting weights in the usual place. My older brother Tosiek was there, too, along with his friends. Ten years earlier, I had been able to lift 110 pounds, while the biggest and strongest boys were lifting 190. They knew that I was lifting weights and becoming stronger, but they had never actually seen me lift. They greeted me and my friend awkwardly, joking about how weak I used to be. Tosiek said, "Show us how strong you've gotten. Maybe we can learn something."

I laughed and knew right away that they still felt superior to me. They were bigger and taller, so they assumed that I would never be able to become stronger than they were. "Sorry," I said, "but we're in a hurry to get to our workout."

"Oh, come on," said a boy who was about 250 pounds and 6-foot-2. He was new to the neighborhood and I had never met him. "Show us. Let's see what the little boy can do."

Having heard that comment, I said: "Okay, load the bar with everything you have." They laughed, but when they saw I was serious, they loaded the bar to 310 pounds. They did not know quite what to make of the situation. They thought I was joking but when I actually approached the bar, everyone fell silent. I lifted the bar to my chest, jerked it above my head, where I held it for a second and then dropped it to the ground. The weights sank about three inches into the earth. They all stood there quietly for about ten seconds, after which they began to express their disbelief. "You really became a small giant," one of them said.

"Unbelievable," my brother said, not trusting his eyes. He went over to the bar and tried to pick it up but it was too heavy for him. He was unable to lift it off the ground. Then one after another, the largest boys tried and all failed. They stood there in amazement, struggling to comprehend what had just happened.

It was not so much the amount of weight that I had lifted that separated us, as it was the time invested that made the difference in weightlifting ability. Any of these boys could easily have achieved what I did, but only if they had been willing to do what I had done: to commit to at least five years of training with a weightlifting coach. That would have seemed overwhelming to them and was not a commitment they would have been willing to make.

They approached me to shake my hand and offer me words of respect. My original goal, however, had changed. I no longer saw my goal relative to the neighborhood bullies. My new goal was the Olympics and I trained very hard to achieve this goal. In 1977, however, just three years before the Moscow Olympics, while doing short squats with 700 pounds, I relaxed my abdominals and I wobbled. My L5 (lumbar five vertebra) moved forward and bruised my spinal column, leaving me paralyzed for two months. My doctor said that the spine would heal and I would be healthy again, but he suggested I retire from weightlifting.

I immersed myself in books as I prepared for the university. After two months, the feeling in my legs returned and I was able to resume light lifting. Because my recovery was speedy, after four months I was able to lift almost the same amount of weight as I had before my injury. The injury almost repeated itself, however. Fortunately, I was able to predict the wobble and I dropped the weights. Afraid of being paralyzed permanently, I decided to follow a long road toward my recovery, training for strength instead of just power.

I read hundreds of books about sports injuries and recovery. As the years passed, my pain and the memory of the injury almost vanished. I added a lot of muscle and my body became bigger. In five years, my weight shot from 130 to 190. In 1993, after immigrating to the U.S. and becoming citizens, Aniela and I found out that the Masters World Weightlifting Championship would be held in Poland in 1997. That would be 20 years after my injury. Aniela persuaded me to take a chance and prepare for the championship. She also asked me to prepare her as well. But first we needed to lose weight. Aniela would need to lose 32 pounds and I would need to lose 60 pounds. We began intense training and in 1995 we entered the Pan American Games. Aniela won first place, while I came in second. In 1996, we qualified for the World Weightlifting Championship in Canada. Again, Aniela won first place and I came in second. The next year, we qualified for The World Weightlifting Championship in Poland. Aniela and I both came in first place. I stood on the podium with my right hand on my chest. My heart pounded when the American flag was raised and the national anthem of the U.S. was played. From the podium where I stood, I looked out toward the audience, where my two weightlifting friends sat, sharing our happiness. We were interviewed by various journalists and we were nicknamed "The Golden Couple." Thirty years after I had begun my weightlifting journey, my dream had come true.

Goals are essential in life. The longer it takes to achieve them, the more meaningful they are. To create a plan, one needs goals. Because of the plan, all kinds of different strategies are created as well. Your goal may be distant but the drive to achieve it must be constant and strong. The farther away the goal is, the more intense the pursuit becomes. And when you encounter difficulties, they can be overcome by the love you develop over the years for your dream. When you deal with a difficult and lengthy pursuit, you educate yourself. Your confidence that you can achieve anything is created. You become wise, compassionate and ready to mentor others.

WHERE MOUNTAINS BEGIN TO RISE

Mary came back from Hawaii
where she attended an inspirational
retreat. For three days she
listened and finally learned
how to move mountains.

When I saw her she said, "I don't understand
how I could have been so weak
and unable to follow that simple diet.
I must have been depressed,
or something else clouded my mind"

Mary was high as if she was on drugs.
She spoke by herself the whole hour
moving on the couch constantly and
making her eyes bigger whenever she said
how the past was impossible and far away.

She left with her chest high and proud.
Watching, I thought, "Just three days in Hawaii.
There's nothing she can't achieve."

One week later when I opened the door
Mary stood on the porch with her chest collapsed
as she stared at the floor while saying hello.
She walked over and slouched on the couch.

We did not talk for five minutes. Then
she lifted her head and looked
straight into my eyes:
"I was perfect for three days
before I began eating.

Today I am six pounds heavier, but a week ago
I thought I would be six pounds lighter.
I was so inspired but now
I'm even scared to think of what's coming next."

"Welcome back."
"Welcome back?" she asked.
"Yes, welcome back to the place
where mountains begin to rise."

CHAPTER 4

Pursuit

Desire is the key to motivation, but it's determination and commitment to an unrelenting pursuit of your goal—a commitment to excellence—that will enable you to attain the success you seek.

—Mario Andretti

Journey into the Joy of Practice

There is a saying in Polish, "Podroze ksztalca." In addition to twisting your tongue, the phrase may be translated as, "Travel broadens your horizons." Or simply – educate.

Jerzy and I travel a lot and we love it. We always have, either in the form of camping trips to Joshua National Park, visiting friends and family in Poland, Germany or Canada, or simply exploring some places that we think are worth seeing like Lourdes in France or ancient Native American ruins at Mesa Verde in Colorado. We use our free time to do that, often inviting good friends to go along with us good friends, because when you are together in a car for hours, you either have a fantastic time or a miserable one if you pick the wrong companions.

Eight years ago, we moved to Northern California, leaving behind our established business and friends of eighteen years. The combination of new home, new business situation and new daughter prompted us to feel the need for a transition to the new life that we would be creating in a new place. So when our daughter was three weeks old and able to travel, we began to drive back and forth between the San Francisco Bay Area and Los Angeles. Every weekend, we were in LA. During the weekdays in the Bay Area, as we focused on our new clients, our business began to grow.

At first, getting ready for these trips was all about planning, preparation, packing, and so on. Since we had a baby, it was important to take certain things. This often proved to be tiring and frustrating because we either forgot to bring something or we packed so much "just in case" that we felt like sardines in our car. Our friends would look at us as if we were crazy.

Practice makes things easier, so we've learned from experience.

As time went on, we acquired a better sense of what and how much we needed. Packing became easier and we traveled light. Driving became more pleasurable. I would use the time to read, sing and play with our daughter. While she napped, I would read plays to Jerzy that he liked and didn't have time to read during the week. We would listen to books on tape or simply converse.

With this approach, the trips were no longer a chore, something we had to put up with. Instead, we looked forward to them. As our daughter would now say, "Let's go to the rocket!" We did what we liked, not in the comfort of our living room but in our car.

The turning point for us was when we accepted the fact that we needed time in our transitional period to create a new life for ourselves and it was up to us to decide how to deal with that. As we adapted to this new lifestyle, we noticed that time seemed to pass quickly and we felt energized, rather than tired. The stops that we would take became predictable. We slowed down our driving, drove with the flow, not jumping from lane to lane. We would arrive without stress. More importantly, we connected with the joy of being together. Those trips were invaluable for us, the source of book ideas, solutions for our clients and our business. The drive time gave us the luxury of working out many issues.

There was a physical destination to reach but no longer tension in getting there. Our focus was not on what was wrong or bad about the present situation, but how to embrace it and find solutions. After we changed our attitude, we were able to move forward, smoothly and continuously.

Through the years of practice helping people, we noticed that many of our clients were dealing with negative feelings: they lost hope of ever getting better, they focused on what was wrong with the current situation, what was missing in their lives and so on. They were frustrated and disappointed with the smallest challenges and they often quit before small incremental improvements added up to significant changes that would have become evident to them. They reverted back to their old attitudes and habitual ways of thinking, just going through the motions. Old habits became their ghetto, their prison.

What we practice becomes our way of life.

We establish our lifestyle by what we do habitually: exercising daily, meditating, eating cinnamon buns for breakfast, playing piano, going for a walk after dinner, reading books, even talking about others or having negative feelings.

How then should we approach a harmful or negative established ritual, routine, or habit that we either fall into or adopt, but we want to change?

Albert Einstein observed that, "The mind that created the problem is not going to solve the problem."

If there is a need to create an improved lifestyle, one has to adopt a new mindset. What we routinely practice supports the formation of physical and mental habits. The focus must be on what you want, rather than what you don't want.

One example would be to not spend time reading books about getting fat, which will only teach you about why and how we get fat. Knowing how one becomes fat does not mean you know how to become lean. If you want to get lean, find books that can teach you how, and people who can inspire and motivate you along the journey. If you want to become positive, search for positive inspirational books and surround yourself with positive people.

Accepting the reality that the process is going to be a journey is the first step. There also will be bumps on the road, which will not prevent you from getting where you want to go if you keep going.

To illustrate the change, I would like to tell a story about a man who was very mean. As he was approaching his 40th birthday, he realized that he had no friends and his family wanted nothing to do with him. His boss and coworkers tolerated him only because he delivered quality work. The realization of the situation left him with feelings of loneliness and depression.

After recognizing that it was up to him to change he decided to do something about it. He sought out a spiritual master and asked him whether he could still change and, if so, how he could accomplish this. The master, after listening, instructed the man to do seven nice things for others and return in one week.

The man was puzzled but followed the master's instructions, searching daily for the opportunity to do nice things for others. The next morning, he held the elevator door for a woman who was rushing to catch it. The following day, he brought a cup of coffee for his secretary, who looked at him suspiciously. He made himself write a birthday card to his brother. And so things continued for the next few days.

After the week was up, the man returned to the spiritual master, eager to report his good deeds. The master, however, was not interested in listening. He told him to keep doing the same things for the next several weeks.

This sequence continued for several months. Eventually, the man complained: "I don't feel any different. Will I ever change?"

"I already see the changes in you," the master said. "You are not the same person who first came to me."

What counts in a process of change is the doing, not the thinking or talking about change. Practice will eventually make you into a new you. You have to define what is it that you want to practice to become. Then just follow the practice.

Results

Whatever we do in life, we want results. The most depressing scenario is to spend time and money and not achieve them. Why does this happen to us, even though it's clear what we want? It reminds me of Einstein saying, "Insanity: doing the same thing over and over again and expecting different results." There must be an answer as to why we Americans spend more money than any country in the world on health and fitness and we get worse every year instead of getting better. Let's explore how we fall into Einstein's saying and correct that derailing mistake.

Mary is common example. She is in her forties and was told by her doctor that her pre-diabetes and frail immune system was the result of her being overweight and weak. The prescription would be to lose weight and get stronger. Hearing this, Mary sighed with relief. She thought she had something more serious like cancer or chronic fatigue, but she got lucky—just overweight and weakness. She should be able to fix this in no time; after all, losing weight and getting strong was a trivial matter, anyone could do it.

Mary thought about doing it by herself, but her friends for some reason advised her to get professional help. The next morning, she appeared at the local gym, where she hired a personal trainer who was going to help her to lose all the fat and get stronger. She bought twenty personal sessions, assuming that would be enough. At 6am she checked in at the gym and was told that her trainer would see her shortly. Jack came ten minutes late, but it did not bother her at all because when she saw him, Mary was speechless. Jack was tall and built like a Greek God, with tanned skin and a six-pack stomach. He was beautiful. After he introduced himself he told her that they would get to business right away so nobody wasted time. He placed her on a treadmill and showed how to use it. As she started jogging, he began telling her about his life—where he was born, where he'd lived and how he became a trainer. One hour passed very quickly. Mary felt fantastic. She thought that if working out was like this, then she would gladly do it forever. She loved the trainer, she loved the music, and she loved the whole atmosphere. It was simply lovely. After the treadmill they went to a bench, where Jack helped her do some bench presses followed by pull downs. Jack explained to her that they would use the most sophisticated and contemporary training technique called muscle confusion. Every day she will be training different a muscle group with different intensity, so the muscle would never know what was going on. In this way she would boost her metabolic rate, lose all the fat and get very strong. Mary was in heaven: she would lose all the weight, get stronger, and be entertained!

But results must be the results of an everyday plan that is developed to reach set goals. Today the goal is to go to a gym and work out, or to have different workouts spread throughout the week: Yoga on Monday, weightlifting on Tuesday, Pilates on Wednesday, and so on. Of course, the result of this kind of activity is really just activity by itself or pure entertainment. Weeks passed, and then months, and one day Mary visited her doctor again, who told her, "Mary what are you doing? You are 5 pounds heavier and your sugar level got higher."

"But I go to a gym everyday and I even have a personal trainer!"

Her doctor knew that he needed to help Mary understand, so he softened his voice and said, "Look Mary, going to a gym is not enough. Your workout has to make you lose weight and make you stronger, whether in a gym or at home, or with a trainer or without one. Let's meet in a month and see if you find your way to a lifestyle with a focus on results, not on entertainment."

Mary was lucky. She found The Happy Body by searching the internet. She bought the book and started the program: the same exercise routine every day, done mindfully with a singular focus to improve strength and agility over time. Eating every three hours, mostly vegetables and protein to flood the body with nutrients to stabilize blood sugar levels. Meditative music after every workout to calm the mind and increase willpower. Everything opposite to what she was doing before.

She returned to her doctor after a month. When he saw that he didn't even need to measure her, he knew she was getting the results she needed. He was happy and he shouted, "Mary you look fantastic!" Mary did not have to hide her emotions, she was happy too. After he measured her, he told her that she had lost ten pounds and her blood sugar level had dropped from 130 to 85. He told her that she didn't have to take drugs—the results were better than he had expected. "Tell me, how did you do it" he said. And she told him the story.

The most important principle in life is to get results, but to achieve results you need goals, a plan, and the right execution. If, after one month, your progress is not showing clear results, then change your approach completely. Fire your trainer, nutritionist, business coach, the art teacher— whoever is supposed to help you to get results. Don't waste your time on entertainment when you really want results.

EVERYTHING WORKS

One day my friend told me,
It doesn't work.
Is there anything in life
that doesn't work? I answered.
He looked at me, smiling.
There are many things that don't work.
For example, I'm trying to lose
weight but it doesn't work.

What happens? I asked.
I get stuck, my friend.
Then you know… I told him.
What do I know?
Being stuck works.
My friend laughed and said,
It's so easy to miss.

CHAPTER 5

Ascend

Without a struggle, there can be no progress.

—Frederick Douglass

Transitions: From Break feast to Breakfast

One month before our daughter Natalie was born,
we moved from Southern to Northern California.
Everything was new to us: a new baby and a new house
with many old things to replace and fix. Also, there
was our new practice to develop from the bottom up.
We didn't have any family here in the States so we were
coping all by ourselves. It was not easy. We needed help.

Then I found out that my brother Ted, a carpenter,
who lives in Poland, lost his job. We sent an invitation
for him to come and help us out. The timing was right
for him as well as for us; we welcomed him gratefully.
His delayed flight arrived at the San Francisco airport in
the evening. We collected his luggage and drove home,
all of us exhausted, including the baby. We had a glass of
champagne to welcome Ted and went right to bed.

Next morning our energy was great. I put the kettle
on for our tea and set the table for breakfast. I arranged
some of our morning bars in a basket together with some
Men's Bread, freshly made peanut and almond butter and
warm soy milk for the tea. We were sitting and sipping
tea, enjoying our healthy food bars. Ted took one look at
the table, visibly surprised.

"That's your breakfast?"

"Yes," I answered. "If you would like something
else you're welcome to help yourself to anything in the
kitchen."

He made himself scrambled eggs with tomatoes and
onion. Then he ate some Men's Bread with jam, followed
with yogurt with banana and blueberries. He was hungry

and eager to start his work. Later the same day we went grocery shopping. I told Ted to choose whatever he wanted. Soon, our shopping cart was filled up with eggs, bacon, waffles, pancake mix, jams, whole milk, yogurt, different kind of chesses, deli meats, sausage, fruit, pastry, sourdough bread, rolls. He looked so happy I didn't want to say anything.

"Tomorrow, I will make breakfast for you," he said eagerly.

Next morning we woke up to the smell of fried bacon, eggs and freshly brewed coffee. Our dining table looked like a feast for at least ten people. There were scrambled eggs with strips of bacon on our plates. In the middle of the table there was a stack of buttermilk pancakes with a bowl of mixed berries next to it. There was also a plate with different kind of deli meats and cheeses, and a basket of bread and rolls. Ted looked at us with pride.

"Sit down, eat," he said, helping himself to all of it.

"Well," Jerzy said. "Thank you Ted, but we don't eat like this. The way we like to eat is simple, without overeating. Otherwise we feel sluggish, and have less energy to digest all this food. Our food bar, or a piece of hemp bread with almond butter, or a cup of Greek yogurt with some berries satisfies us. This actually gives us more energy for things like writing, training, and helping our clients, plus it frees up time for just having more fun."

We felt that at this moment there was no way to persuade him without hurting his feelings. We watched his expression shift from happy and proud to angry and hurt.

For the next few weeks he didn't say much, but we watched how Ted's breakfast was changing.

At first he would wake up early to make hot meals like scrambled eggs with toast, then the next thing was oatmeal with some fruit, then dry cereal with milk and a cup of coffee.

Then one morning Jerzy woke up and Ted was already sitting at the table, a cup of tea in front of him and a bar in his hand.

"Not bad," Ted said.

"Yeah, it's pretty good," Jerzy replied.

After some months he started to analyze his old lifestyle and habits, comparing them to what he had learned in our house.

"Every morning I used to go to the store to buy fresh rolls, milk, eggs, and butter. There were lines at the grocery store so I was always rushing back home. Then I'd cook and clean up, but I always felt heavy afterwards. I'd fall asleep on the tramway on the way to work. I never realized I could feel differently."

He never put these things together, that it was food that was making him feel slow and tired. And it was a habit that he never questioned. His first reaction was anger.

"Why did I waste so much time?" he asked. "Instead of overspending, getting fatter, not feeling good, I could have had a piece of bread with nut butter or yogurt with fruit. Simple. If I count all the hours I spent on chores related to food, and imagine those hours I could have been working, and making money! I would have had savings! I wouldn't have had to leave my family, either." He was devastated.

"How could I have wasted so much time and energy?"

"You didn't know better," I said to him.

I watched Ted applying efficiency when he worked on his projects; planning, comparing, preparing. He used his logic and math skills. He was a good craftsman. But when it came to his health, he never looked at the way he lived life, how his habits and likes and daily routines actually affected his income and his body. He was not efficient when it came to his lifestyle.

When he went back home, he was forty pounds lighter, straightened up — literally— and equipped with three boxes of healthy food bars. He was "handy and handsome," as one of our friends said. And she wasn't the only one who noticed the change in him. He left with great enthusiasm to help his own family to get better, and he had all the tools in his hands.

It will be natural for anyone who starts doing something new or different to go through transitions on the way. There are many reasons for our attachments, like culture, customs, habits, beliefs, level of education, "bandwagons," and so on. New and different means you will eventually become someone new and different. It is easier if you have a role model, someone who will inspire, motivate and help you to transition to a new place. With my brother Ted, we didn't teach but we exposed him to our lifestyle, and eventually he understood and embraced a new way of living. There are mentors, coaches and teachers who dedicate their lives to help others become the best they can be. They look for solutions, for transitions to attain the next level. The emphasis must be on efficiency, where effort equals results. Look at what you're doing now and ask yourself a question: is what I'm doing bringing the expected results?

Progress

There can be no change without progress. You might be going to gyms, taking the classes you like without thinking about long-term progress regarding your health and fitness. You find the classes entertaining, but, as the years pass, you age and become increasingly overweight. You develop inexplicable pains and become weaker. All the things you did to help yourself in the past no longer work. This puzzles you, so you ask others about it but they are in the same situation. You notice that your body needs more time to rest and everything is becoming more difficult, even the things that in the past you were able to do easily.

As you search for answers, you learn that aging begins after thirty-five. From that point it proceeds at a pace of about two percent every year. So you are told that if you want to maintain your current level of strength, you have to improve by two percent a year, just to break even. To improve two percent annually, you increase the length of your exercise. But you still get worse over time or you get more pains and you are unable to exercise for the same period. To understand what is really happening, you need to examine the conditions and the type of progress you're making. That way, you will not engage in exercises or activities that are counterproductive.

There are three kinds of progress: acquisitional, cyclical, and skill development.

Think back to the time when you collected baseball cards or stamps or anything else. When you added something to your collection, it always grew larger. It made no difference when you added it. After adding another item, you had always had a larger collection, unless you sold or lost something. So collective progress does not depend on time; we have more whenever we add something.

The next type of progress does not depend on time, but does not last forever. Whenever you go to a hairdresser, your appearance improves dramatically and then slowly fades as the days and weeks go by. One day you look so bad that you return to the hairdresser to get yourself cleaned up again. The same thing happens when we go to a make-up artist or manicurist. Of course, any great improvement that you can achieve almost immediately does not last forever. We're able to enjoy becoming beautiful almost instantly.

Progress in skill depends on time and it is achieved through the body's adaptation to a higher level of intensity or stress. This progress is necessary when we want to become better artists or athletes—or to improve in terms of any other activity that cannot be advanced without practice. If you want to get better at playing piano, then you have to practice. If you stop practicing, especially for an extended period of time, you regress. Improvement happens when we are consistent and engage in extensive practice. What this means is that every time you practice, you pay total attention to whatever you are doing, intensifying slightly more than the day before. For example, if you bend forward with your knees locked and cannot touch the floor, you need to practice touching the floor each day, until one day, you manage to touch it. Sometimes, it may seem that you are not progressing at all. Subtle changes happen in your body, however, which accumulate the needed skill over time. One day, you are finally able to reach the floor and, to your surprise, touch it. This is a quantum change.

When I was twenty, I could not power clean 235 pounds to my chest. As months passed, I managed to break all the projected records, except for the one relating to power clean. For some reason, I could not break this one. I told my coach that something must be wrong with my lifting. "It will happen," the coach said. "Just keep practicing." Nine months passed and nothing changed but my coach kept saying that it would happen. I just needed to keep practicing. One day a year later, when I went with my friend Jack to the gym, the bar felt different in my hands after warming up. It felt lighter than usual. When the time came to clean 235, I cleaned it as if it were a broom. (When lifts happen effortlessly, we call them broom lifts.) I attempted 240 and that was like a broom, too. The same thing happened with 250 and 255. I only failed at 260. From that day on, I never had a problem lifting 235 pounds.

When we want to improve certain skills, it takes time and practice to create enough changes in the body for the skill to develop. Also, the better we become, the harder it is to break records. We watch figure skaters and gymnasts perform their routines effortlessly, without being conscious of the many hours it took to perfect them. The body needs a certain number of repetitions, always doing the same thing, to get better. If you are patient and practice sufficiently for the time needed, the change will happen.

The Happy Body exercise routine was created to help you achieve the youthfulness of an eighty-year-old world weightlifting champion. When you are in your fifties or sixties, it should be easy for you to achieve this. The most inspiring thing is that there is a big gap between the power of a champion and you, therefore you have a reserve to become better. If, for example, you are a fifty-five-year-old woman and you do not have the energy to sustain a vibrant life, you can change that. Aniela, who is fifty-seven, competes in the 106-pound category. Today, she can still lift 120 pounds over her head, while you can probably lift only 30 pounds, if that much. That's a difference of 300 percent. You could easily get depressed and keep getting weaker. Or you could say: "Wow! That is very inspiring. For my age and weight, I could be a lot of stronger than I am. I could actually become 300 percent stronger."

If you practice The Happy Body for a year, you will become stronger, leaner and more flexible. Otherwise the year will pass, and if you just keep doing whatever you are doing now, you will only get worse. So why not do what has the power to make you better over time? In a year, you will get better. In five years, the results will be incredible.

Progress is possible. You just need to know that and to continue to practice until progress happens. The biggest challenge of all is to permanently sustain a desirable lifestyle.

HITTING A WALL

My friend Mary told me,
I hit a wall. She looked as if
she wanted me to tell her why.
Which wall? I asked.
I just can't lose weight.
The scale doesn't budge.
Yes, but which wall did you hit? I asked again.
Well, she said, maybe it was
too many pancakes on Thursdays,
and on Fridays
too many glasses of wine.

She was smiling.

You know, I told her,
The last time I heard this phrase
was in Poland in 1969
when I went to high school.
My father told me that
after World War II
a Warsaw University professor came
to teach his first lesson and said,
"We hit a wall.
The Germans came to take
our bodies and stayed
for six years,
but then the Russians came
to take our souls
and they will stay for a long time
before we break this wall."

When I was done speaking
Mary dropped her smile.
She spoke softly.

I'd better go now, she said,
and take my wall down,
pancake by pancake.

CHAPTER 6

Knowing

Do you want to know who you are? Don't ask. Act! Action will delineate and define you.

—Thomas Jefferson

Principles in Life: Finding Your Own

It was late October, the sky was pure blue and the sun was shining brightly. On days like this, our family feels lucky to live in California, where even in winter, we can enjoy summer-like outdoor activities. We all agreed that it was a perfect day to spend at the beach, our favorite past time on the weekends. There is something calming about watching the rolling of the waves, listening to the sound of the water crashing on the rocks, punctuated occasionally by a seagull's cry breaking the spell of tranquility. It helps us slow down, bringing body and mind into the present. It makes us feel rejuvenated in a short period of time.

We each have our favorite things to do at the beach. I love walking barefoot, as the sand massages my feet. Our daughter enjoys drawing giant faces with a stick on the wet sand or designing houses (prompting Jerzy's prediction about Natalie becoming an architect when she grows up). It is also fun to work together, creating forts from driftwood, then planting gardens around them with shells, rocks and seaweed. Of course, Jerzy is always up for a short nap in the sun after all this hard work. The beach relaxes and refreshes us like no other place.

This particular day, the air coming through the car window was strangely both warm and crisp as we drove toward the beach. We were all in a good mood. It was early afternoon on a Saturday and we expected a smooth drive. After driving for a few minutes, we came to a sudden stop. As far as we could see, there were cars in front of us and we were on a one-lane road with nowhere to turn around. It looked like we were stuck. The pre-Halloween festivities held in Half Moon Bay contributed to the traffic jam, we later learned.

There was nothing else to do but to move along with the traffic, to inch forward. I put on a CD with our favorite stories and started looking out the window at the passing scenery. Because we moved very slowly, I realized that I hadn't noticed many details about this road even though we'd passed this way hundreds of times before. Most striking to me was that the sides of the road were filled with plastic bags clasping the bushes, empty bottles reflecting light, paper bags and colorful wrappers strewn among the rocks. "Oh, my God," I said. "Look at all this garbage outside. I cannot believe that I didn't notice it before." It is not possible to see all of that when you drive 40 or 50 miles an hour in the hermetically sealed capsule of a car. I had to slow down and open the window in order to see it.

"Would you throw anything outside the car window?" I asked my daughter.

"Garbage? No!" Her response was definite and firm.

"If you asked me, that's not my way, either," said my husband.

It would not cross my mind to keep my car clean at the expense of the outdoors.

We started to talk about the process of littering. Starting with a single piece of trash, it is just a matter of time before things begin to pile up. There are people who would never litter, who care about the environment and adhere to principles. And then there are people who simply follow. When the environment is clean, they are clean. When it is littered, they contribute to the litter. They follow the precedent. I understand the efforts of many people and organizations that pick up litter along roads, beaches and parks. They follow the "broken window" theory.

This idea was introduced by two social scientists, James Q. Wilson and George L. Kelling, whose theory has been used to support reforms in the area of criminal policy in social behavior. They conducted numerous experiments involving graffiti, abandoned buildings and abandoned cars, with regard to what creates change.

In one of the experiments, they observed what happened over time to an abandoned building in New York City. Originally, there were no broken panes in any of the windows. Hundreds of people would pass by each day and nothing happened. Then, one day, glass in a single window was broken. This attracted a group of boys who shattered other windows. The building started to look abandoned, attracting homeless people. Then gangs used the place for target practice, drinking, and other undesirable activities. Within a short period of time, the building had become vandalized. People who lived nearby started to take a longer route to drive home, in order to avoid it. The condition of the building began to spread to the surrounding community.

Could such a situation be avoided? The researchers discovered that to prevent vandalism is to fix problems when they are small. In the case of a broken window, this would be simply be a matter of fixing the window by replacing the glass. Other similar experiments proved that it helped to erase graffiti, prevent the theft of car parts when a car sits at the curb, stop the accumulation of garbage on sidewalks, and so on. If these situations are not attended to, the problems snowball.

As we continued driving, we discussed the "broken window" phenomenon, applying it to lifestyle, a subject of interest to us. How do we compromise our efforts when it comes to following a healthy and fit lifestyle? It is easier to be bad than good. We need to be forced to be good. That's why laws are necessary. Without a small number of individuals who initiated the actions that led to the passage of legislation, today we would still have slavery, women would not have the right to vote and smoking would still be allowed on planes.

Whatever happens is culture. As a society, we evolve, adapt, change. There is a term in psychology, "cultural obesity," which describes how environment influences lifestyle. Let's say you live in a low-income neighbor-hood where there are no trees on your street. There is a park, but to get there you have to pass many drunkards and homeless people. You might even see gangs dealing drugs. So your choices about how to spend free time become limited. You end up, as everyone does, either in front of a computer or a TV. Role modeling is very important. You imitate what you see. What's familiar brings comfort, what's known becomes the accepted way. And that's how it becomes a lifestyle we adopt.

I suppose we all may find areas in our lives where we create the opportunity to activate the "broken window" rule. It doesn't have to be throwing trash out of your car window. It can be as simple as overeating or not exercising. I call it the "criminal mind," the one that emerges when no one else is watching us. The "principled mind," on the other hand, is the one that upholds moral values, prompting us to act ethically, without the threat of punishment, without someone watching over us.

The buffet is one of the places that gives rise to the temptation to "break windows," by overeating or choosing the wrong foods. Buffets are designed in part like casinos: to lure people into doing what the creators of the establishment want them to do, at the expense of their own best interests. The colors, the sounds, the layout: everything is deliberately designed with this in mind. For many of us, temptation is stronger than willpower and nobody can stop us but ourselves. The personal habits that we learned and established over a lifetime are not easy to change.

If you want to transform yourself for the better, what do you need to do?

Having a set of strong principles definitely helps compel us to become healthy and fit. That is how THB Program works. Once you begin to follow a set of healthy principles, food becomes a source of nourishment and rejuvenation for the body. It may be difficult initially to like what's good for us, such as drinking vegetable juices or eating frozen yogurt with probiotics instead of ice cream. If we eat sugary, salty and fatty foods, vegetable juices are hard to enjoy. They might seem "medicinal" but actually that is what good food should be: good medicine for the body. Similarly, exercise helps to keep the body strong and flexible the same way that the daily relaxation practice releases stress.

As we declutter our lives, we have less on our minds. This enables us to slow down and focus on what is important. We need to see in what areas of our lives we overdo or don't do enough, and how that happens. With time and practice, we are able to develop within ourselves a kind of internal, objective observer, who guides us toward making good choices with regard to food and exercise. In this way, we are able to progress from being reactive to proactive. Glimpses of awareness enable us to gather feedback about what we repeatedly do that is undesirable for us. Then we can start to implement behavioral changes, to stop being mindless and to stop defeating the desired outcome.

The sushi master in the movie Jiro Dreams of Sushi said, "You have to eat good food to serve good food." The same applies to exercise: There is bad exercise and there is good exercise. Bad exercises can wear out cartilage and cause loss of muscle, the retention of which is vital to aging youthfully.

The Happy Body Program is implemented using simple guidelines: A workout routine that over time makes people strong, flexible and fast, while improving posture and adding muscle mass. A food plan that nurtures and rejuvenates the body. A daily stress release technique that helps us be focused and mindful about our choices, guiding us toward a life that is simple and efficient.

In the cultivation of these practices, we discovered that there is, in addition to the "broken window" rule, an "unbroken window" rule. This was brought to our attention by a psychologist client of ours.

She had been struggling with overeating and being overweight for most of her life. At first we asked her to keep a journal that we designed along the lines of the "broken window" theory. We called it "45 Happy Body Check Points." She was going to follow five key directives of THB: (1) daily food intake (two meals and three snacks), (2) time of eating (every three hours, with the kinds of foods described in the plan), (3) volume (adjusted individually), (4) daily exercise routine and (5) relaxation (five minutes daily with music and lavender oil). If she was faithfully following the plan, she would receive the highest score of 45 points: 15 points for food intake (covering points 1-3 above), 15 points for exercise and 15 points for relaxation. Each category had two images, one of a broken window and another of an unbroken window. She simply had to circle one: broken when she broke the principles, unbroken when she followed them. Each day, she recorded her point totals.

After a week, we learned where she was failing. She loved to exercise, so she exercised every day and that made her feel great. No broken window there. She was inconsistent with the relaxation, however, and she internalized it as a "waste of time" because it seemed too passive. Once she lay down, her mind started to race and the list of "things to take care of" and "to do" started forming in her head. This was very disturbing and the opposite of what she expected from relaxation. She still tried from time to time, but was inconsistent in her practice. That is, until she realized how regular relaxation practice made her more focused and mindful about her choices with regard to food, timing and volume.

When we reviewed her record of food intake, we found some patterns that she followed, unknowingly, until she started to record them. She had problems with type of food, volume and time (the practice of eating in three-hour intervals to avoid ups and downs in blood sugar level). Through observation, she learned how she would stop one of her old habits only to replace it with a new one that was not helping her make any progress in her weight loss.

But as weeks and months passed, she was more and more aligned with practicing THB program. After some time, she had the experience of finally achieving an "unbroken window," that is, following all the principles of The Happy Body—100%—for the first time.

She told us how this happened at a dinner party where there was nothing to eat that would fit her food plan. Usually she would just eat whatever was being offered. This time she consciously examined the choices: penne pasta with rich meat sauce, Italian bread with garlic butter, and butter lettuce salad with creamy dressing and croutons. There was also pound cake and ice cream for desert. As difficult as it was, she decided not to eat there, but rather to wait until she got home. She noticed that many times, she almost gave in, watching other people enjoying eating. She was experiencing a range of feelings: the feeling of being deprived, anti-social, joyless. But each time, she reminded herself that she was not really hungry. She had eaten a snack before coming to the party. After two hours of struggling, she felt physically exhausted. She left the party earlier than she had originally planned. As she drove home, she realized that she had been faithful to her original intention to not touch the food that was not part of her plan. A wave of energy suddenly swept through her body. She felt energized, as if she had endured something "like climbing a mountain." It was difficult, but she didn't give up; she climbed all the way to see the beautiful view from the top. She felt that all her efforts were worthwhile. This experience allowed her to predict her thoughts and behavior, formulating a plan and strategizing to stay on track. That was the beginning of her journey toward a new and happier self.

When we were moving from L.A. to the San Francisco Bay Area, we decided that Jerzy would drive a U-Haul moving van and I would drive our truck, which we filled with electronics, art, fragile things and our two cats and parakeets.

The day of the move, things were packed in boxes, waiting for Jerzy to come pick them up with the truck. I waited and waited. The rental place was maybe three blocks from where we lived, so I was a little impatient about getting started, as we had many hours of driving ahead of us. Then I began to be concerned. Finally, Jerzy arrived. Before I actually saw him, I heard the screeching of the brakes, the friction of tires, as he tried to park the van in front of our apartment. It took him some time to park it before he came up, all sweaty and obviously stressed out from the short trip.

"I don't think I will be able to drive this dragon," he said. "I've never driven a stick shift and a van as long as this one. It's a different kind of driving. It requires practice that I don't have time for now." We decided that we had to find someone else to do the driving for us. We went back to U-Haul and were told that there was no one who could help us. We were stuck. After a while, a very pleasant Hispanic clerk in his twenties, who was helping us purchase packing supplies at the counter, saw our frustration and, taking pity on a pregnant woman, came up with an idea. He would drive the moving van and his nephew would follow in his car, so that afterwards they could drive back together to LA. But he needed to be at work the next morning. It was an opportunity for them to earn a week's worth of extra cash.

After the store closed, Jesus and his nephew followed us all the way to the Bay Area, with two stops: the first at an In & Out Burger and the second one at a Starbucks. We invited them to order whatever they wanted but to our surprise, they shared just a single burger and fries, with a few sips of lemon water. I asked them why they ate so little and Jesus explained that being hungry was actually helping him stay alert. And, if he drank too much, he would have to make additional restroom stops. He didn't want to take time away from driving and risk being late for work the next day.

We make decisions based on who we are, which is based on our past history, our established thought processes, our habits, emotional intelligence, culture, education and so on. This means that if we don't have a new script or plan, we will just repeat our old one, our past, and nothing is going to change for us.

A Plan

I lived in a small town in Poland called Stargard, which
for the preceding century had belonged to Germany.
My parents were relocated there after World War II and
I was born there in 1954. When my parents arrived,
there were only empty buildings after the Germans
had abandoned the city. In theory, my parents could
have chosen any house to live in, it but some areas were
too dangerous. There were roving, armed gangs that
were robbing and killing people in their newly occupied
houses. Living in an apartment surrounded by other
apartments where railroad workers lived was a relatively
safe option. My parents found such a place, with two
bedrooms and intact glass windows. This latter feature
was very important, as broken-out windows (which many
places had) would make it impossible to keep warm
during the cold winters. There were hundreds of families
living in these three- or four-story buildings. The end of
the war brought the arrival of new children, who added
cheer and renewed energy to the community.

My parents, like everyone else, lived from day to day.
There was never enough money at the end of the month
to feed the children. During that time of scarcity, one
particular family, the Sochacki family, was a frequent
topic of conversation between my parents and their
neighbors.* They had three daughters, one of whom was
a friend of mine. As a child, it was clear to me that my
parents and the neighbors did not like the family and
usually talked about them in a way that was negative and

*Note this is the same story detailed in "Why Are We Poor," from
  another perspective.)

demeaning. They said things like "Those poor children have to eat their bread without butter" and "They're starving their children in order to save money to take with them to their graves." I had a sense of safety and security, knowing that I had parents who cared for me and had my best interests at heart. I felt sad about my friend Grazyna.

As the years passed, the neighborhood children who finished elementary school went on to learn a trade and began working. The three daughters of the Sochacki family, however, took a different path in life. One after another, they went on to attend the most prestigious high school in the city. The gossip that had surrounded them was now replaced by silence. People stopped talking about terrible parents who were starving their children. One day, the news that one daughter had been accepted to a university to study medicine spread like wildfire throughout the community. My parents and neighbors were angry. "Who do they think they are? They think their shit rises." They bitterly pronounced, "She'll be back soon. You'll see. Nobody from families like ours can be a doctor."

When I was six years old, my mother and I walked to a nearby farmers' market to buy vegetables for dinner. We stopped at a bookstore and looked at a display window filled with new books.

After a moment of silence my Mother asked me, "So, what would you like to be when you grow up?"

I didn't hesitate. "I will be an engineer and a pilot," I said.

"You will need to study a lot," she said. "Nobody goes to a college without effort."

"I'm ready."

My Mother looked at me with a smile and I think she was proud and happy. I would be her first child to reach this level of knowledge—so distant and yet so close. All I needed was to study and pass the entry exams. During the time I lived in Poland all schools were free, so only belief prevented people from achieving the highest level of education. But first I had to finish elementary school, pass an entry exam for high school and then another one for college four years later. I was ready and couldn't wait for school to begin.

The eight years went by very quickly. I liked math, chemistry and physics so it was easy for me to pass the exam for the most prestigious high school in our city. After I was accepted I felt good about myself. I was in the same school the three daughters attended. My mother was happy, too, although she did not express her happiness when my father was present.

The first week of classes passed very quickly. With the second week came the realization of what was for me an unbearable truth. Almost all the other students were more advanced than I was. Their parents, most of whom had college degrees, had helped them prepare for school even before it began, while I was just partying. The gap was obvious.

Over the next two weeks, I was getting Cs and Fs, while almost everyone else was getting As and Bs. After a month, during Russian class the teacher asked me for my homework, which of course I didn't have, so she gave me an F. Then she asked me for my notebook, which of course I didn't have either, so she gave me another F. Then she asked me to read a paragraph in Russian for which I got another F, and then she asked something in Russian which I didn't understand so one more F and, to finish her performance, she asked me to spell a word so she could give me yet another F. I received five F's in ten minutes. I just sat there without having any idea what the whole thing meant. I looked around and I saw my friends, who could not comprehend what had just happened either.

I was increasingly aware of being the target of jokes. Eventually, when I could no longer bear the situation, I stopped going to the prestigious high school and signed up for trade school, to become a locksmith. Here the situation was the opposite: I was an A student while others were getting Fs. But that didn't make me feel better. I knew that there were others, elsewhere, much better than I, which made me increasingly depressed. When we got paid at the end of the month, I would go with others for a drink, usually beer or wine. As the months went by, I was drinking more and more—until six months later, I was expelled from trade school.

Thus began my life as an alcoholic. Every day, I would leave the house and meet up with others like me. Together, we foraged for money to buy beer, wine or vodka. At the end of the day, I would come home drunk, and I would wake up the next morning without remembering half of the previous day. Sometimes I lost two or three days in a row, leaving home on a Friday and coming back on a Monday, thinking it was a Saturday. Thoughts of despair became more frequent and pronounced but I did not have the strength to stop them. I felt as if I was having an out-of-body experience, watching things from a distance.

After my troubled years, when I finally became sober, I was nineteen without a high school education and without a profession. In the meantime, Grazyna finished high school and also was accepted to study medicine.

One day I was looking out my window and saw Grazyna pass by, taking a walk. I came out of the house and joined her. When she saw me she smiled happily and said, "How are you? I heard that you stopped drinking. I am so happy for you."

"Thank you," I said, but I heard the great news that you were accepted to the university to study medicine."

"Yeah. I am very happy. But I have to tell you that I was not expecting to get in."

"Well, you deserve it. I know how hard you studied. I haven't seen you at all during these last few years."

She looked at me and smiled, "You know that it didn't happen because of me, don't you?"

"Sure, I know," I said.

"What will you do now? Do you have any plan?"

"I will probably go into the army." We were now back at her apartment building and it was time to say goodbye. Grazyna was leaving for the university the next day.

"I am sure you don't need it, but I will say it anyway. Good luck."

She smiled happily and said, "Thank you," and then added, "I know that you worry, but I want to tell you that I always liked you very much. There was something good in you and I am sure you will find your way back to it. Even my mother liked you, and when you fell into drinking she said once that you were a very nice and promising boy, and that it was so sad what had happened to you. She is happy you stopped."

I felt a strange feeling rushing through my body, something distant and familiar and soothing. "Thanks," I said, "I hope we will see each other more."

"Me too."

I wanted to go, but I still lingered as if I wanted to say something. Grazyna sensed that something was wrong.

"What is it Jerzy? Tell me."

"Well, You're going to study medicine and it's shocking to me. You lived on the same street where nobody ever thought about going to college and now you are going. In five years you will be a doctor, something unreachable to all of us living in this community. We thought that becoming a doctor was only for special people and you're going to be one. How did it happen? Did you plan this?"

"You must be kidding! My mother did. I hated to study when you guys played soccer, but my mother used to say one day you will thank me. Tomorrow I'm going to the university and I'm very happy. The first time I went to see the college it was as if I was in a magic land. Girls and boys everywhere carrying books, talking about what they learned and what they needed to learn. I remember you loved books. You always carried a book with you. What happened?"

It had already been four years since I'd had a book under my arm. "You know I fell into darkness and it seemed there was no way out."

"I'm glad you're out," she said. "Keep in touch with me. Will you?"

"Sure, I will. I hope one day our paths will cross again."

"They will, I know," she said, smiling.

I turned and walked home. I was nineteen with no high school education and my friends were already studying medicine, but I knew if anyone could do it, I could too. I decided that I would graduate from college so I needed to have a plan. I would have to go to high school first, but my brain was now empty so I needed to relearn what I'd forgotten. I decided to study everything in one year and apply the following year to high school. My plan was to study for six hours every day and take the high school exam in May. Every weekend I summarized what I learned and memorized it. Every month I would review everything again. Even though it often was inconvenient to study, especially when my friends were going out for dinner or a party, I stuck to the plan. (Usually I could catch up with my friends anyway, and I found out that I truly wasn't missing anything.)

In May I took the exam. Two weeks later I walked to the high school to find out if I had been accepted. Pages with the names of those who passed were posted on the school billboard. It was exactly five years after I had stood there for the first time searching for my name. I took a deep breath and began to read down the list. All names were alphabetically organized so it did not take long to spot my name in type—Jerzy Gregorek. I stood there with a mixture of contradictory feelings—disappointed, proud, sad, and happy all at once.

Two years later the youngest daughter in Grazyna's family finished high school and was also accepted to study medicine. Two years after that, the oldest daughter graduated from medical school and began working as a doctor in the medical center where my parents and neighbors went for treatment. A year after that, Grazyna came back with a medical degree and two years later the youngest sister became a doctor as well. In the meantime, I finished my high school education and was accepted to the Fire Protection Academy to study fire protection engineering.

You must have a goal to have a plan. My parents did not have a goal for us, so we were not aware that we needed a plan and ended up not pursuing anything. The goal is the source of energy attracting and inspiring the creation of a plan. Once a plan is created, a strategy follows, and progress is possible. Without a plan we are like corks drifting across the ocean floor, wishing the ocean would drop us on a good beach, but for most of us, the opposite is true. In the meantime, others are like boats with a rudder and a compass, sailing through the ocean to the place they want to be. Exercise or trying to lose weight without a plan is like that. You entertain yourself with exercise without a defined goal and hope that you will get better. You eat whenever you want, whatever you want, and hope you will lose weight. Years pass, and you only adjust to the changes by saying, "I must be getting old." Meanwhile others your age are living a fantastic life and of course you have a response to that too: "They either have great genetics or they're rich and can afford to hire expert coaches."

The Happy Body Program was created to provide the goal and the plan. The goal is very clear—the robust, strong, rested, and happy body. The plan is very simple—food choices to control weight, an exercise routine to maintain or restore youthfulness, and relaxation to recover energy and release daily stress. Of course when you have a goal and a plan for how to get there it does not necessarily mean you will get there. Usually getting to our goals is a journey that takes months or even years. During that time unexpected events can happen that were not a part of our plan, so we need to find out how to deal with them to still reach our goal. All the solutions we create on our journey are part of a strategy, helping us follow our plan.

REMEMBER, YOU ARE A BUILDER

Two friends were passing a bank
when one of them said,
Some people build banks
while others rob them.
Which are you?
I like to think of myself as a builder,
but often I think about robbing one.
What about you?
I am just a builder.
No desire to rob a bank, then?
No, but I used to have them
until I met my wife, who asked me,
"What kind of man are you?
Do you wait to work
until your children are hungry?"
That's what she asked?
Yes.
How did you answer?
I need help.
Did you get it?
Time passed, but every morning,
just before I left the house,
she kissed me, gave me the snack
she made and said,
"Remember, you are a builder."

CHAPTER 7

Renewal

We don't even know how strong we are until we are forced to bring that hidden strength forward. In times of tragedy, of war, of necessity, people do amazing things. The human capacity for survival and renewal is awesome.

—Isabel Allende

Can We Create a New Past?

Is it possible to create a new past? If it is, let's look at how the past is created. The past at one point is a distant future, when it arrives becomes present, and then it finally turns into the past. I recognize one concept of the past as the given past, the time of our birth until we grow up, when we don't have much influence on the circumstances of our life. We have no choice where we are born, who our parents are, where we live, the language we speak, etc. The given past is a bit of being lucky, or not. But things are not up to us. Present time is current time. I view it as a present, a gift. It's up to us what we do with it, how we use it. We need help from outside—from our parents and teachers—to start growing and developing a mind that is aware of the future. Mentors open up a child's imagination and possibilities. As Aristotle said, "We are what we repeatedly do. Excellence, then, is not an act, but a habit." Children's activities at one point will help them develop and bring them the desired future.

At a certain age we learn how the world works, and we are aware of choices and that we have them, without the influence of others. We can choose who our friends are, which activities we prefer, what books to read, food to eat, just to name a few of our options. This is when we gain power to choose to create a new past, with our full engagement.

What then distinguishes people who achieve from those who don't? Is it willpower, grit, or greed? Is it mindfulness, or perseverance? The list could go on and on, as with the list of books written on these topics. Do they help? Yes, of course, if we apply the knowledge. But what distinguishes the achiever from the wishful thinker?

Let's look at the scenario of two people who would like to learn some kind of skill—let's say to become a locksmith, or perhaps become a professor. The beginning is always the same: we start by learning simple skills that become more complex, and more complex. Anyone can stop learning at any time, and some do, but some are always reaching for more. It is a process of getting from a place of comfort to the discomfort of the unknown, and repeating the cycle until it becomes integrated into life and part of it. Living life means always choosing more difficult tasks in order to grow.

Awareness and imagination of time passing keeps us focused on purpose, what we would want in the future. But to manifest our intention we need to become the kind of person who knows what he wants and be willing to work for it, embracing all difficulties and overcoming personal weaknesses. When we try, at least we have a chance to become a different, better version of our current self.

To illustrate my point, I will bring in the story of Ray, a middle-aged man who was overweight and had a lower back problem. His vital markers were less than desirable: high blood pressure, hypertension, and high cholesterol were just a few. Simply put, he was aging and aging fast. He was in constant pain and had less energy to sustain his current lifestyle. In the first couple of sessions Ray mentioned that he loved boating and his dream was to own a boat one day. He was saving money for it. Being on a boat is a physical task, however, and he was aware of that. So his dream was dissolving as he was growing older and less capable. In a year though, Ray turned around his health and fitness. He lost eighty pounds, and all his biomarkers started looking good; he started using less medication, and even stopped a few prescriptions. Now his future didn't seem so dim. One weekend he and his partner decided that they were ready to buy a boat. The following week he came back, and with a big smile announced that he really didn't want to own a boat after all. He felt strong, had the stamina for travel and didn't feel like being stuck on a boat. His perspective on life changed with his renewed energy and vision, because his body and mind were healthier and fitter.

So what changed his life so completely within the span of a year? He changed his mind. From a wishful thinker he became a doer, empowered by the education he received about what was possible and what he needed to do to achieve it. He also gained emotional intelligence ¬– he had to make difficult choices, and stay with what he needed to do to achieve his goal.

We are all born equipped with an organ that we call the brain. Its tissue and chemistry dictate the actions and reactions that are encoded, the primitive ones as well as those learned during our lifetime. We have certain genetic predispositions because of our ancestors, so if we are lucky we get good genes…or not so good ones. But a lot of what we do with our brain is up to us. This is where the difference between mind and brain is obvious; the brain is gray and white matter, and the mind is the intellect and intelligence we accumulate throughout our lifetime. Our intelligence creates the self. By educating ourselves through school and other practices and by creating good habits, we develop a better mind.

What we focus on, what we strive to achieve, how we think about the future and materializing it in reality—all this creates an image of what could be. Change cannot happen without you changing your mind, your system of beliefs.

So how do we create a new past, the one we envision, not the one that just happens to us? Once we come to understanding that a lot depends on us, we create the possibility for change. Yet understanding without putting the new knowledge into action, into practice, is useless. We can behave like a car that is parked in a garage, the engine all tuned up, roaring and straining, but the car isn't in gear and doesn't move. It is good to know what the car is capable of; how it works, all the parts and their functions. But the moment we decide to move, we need to get into first gear. And it would also be good to have a roadmap and know the destination. Otherwise we will be cruising around, randomly, hoping that we'll arrive somewhere good. Somehow.

To move forward, we need to change our beliefs, our view on things like food, exercise and renewal. The best approach is to focus on facts, stick with science. Based on facts, the role of science is to confirm a hypothesis through experimentation and verified experience; emotions never come into play. We need to look at facts when we choose to do something like exercise. Or select our food.

"You will never have enough of something you don't want in first place." This is Jerzy's saying that points to the "thing" that we love, maybe love too much, so it becomes an addiction, usually destroying us at the end. If we love food too much, we will develop conditions in the body that will compromise our health, body image, and the quality of our life. There is such a thing as a positive addiction however, where you get hooked on getting better—health-wise, financially, educationally—you want more of a good thing in your life.

In The Happy Body there are three elements that need to work in synchronicity. They are: the food plan, the exercise program and the relaxation techniques. Let's explore some differences within each category:

Exercising vs Training

People exercise, athletes train. What is the difference between these two? We've watched how quickly exercise has become a pastime activity, a kind of pacifier, or just something to do. The worst justification for it is as a punishment for overeating. Exercise as part of a training program has a purpose: it should help your body to be better—stronger, more flexible, faster, more muscular, with improved posture. Athletes who train have clear goals; without them they would simply lose. Without a plan, numbers, or an idea of how you are going to get better, exercise is only a recreational activity where we cruise along, counting on luck instead of intention.

Eating vs Feeding

Eating is an activity, feeding is a conscious act of delivering nutrients with the purpose of growth and survival. Most books written about losing weight or improving body image are based on providing suggestions, offering variety as opposed to simplicity. The more the better. This way you can entertain yourself forever and never achieve health. Relying on an excess of information is counterproductive because it just creates a flood of ideas that distract you from the fact that you need to eat less. To achieve optimal health, you need to know your metabolic rate, your allergies, intolerances, and which foods will help you maintain healthy organs.

Knowledge vs Emotional Intelligence

Simply put, knowledge is information received through education that can be formal or informal. But knowledge without practical application can be useless or even dangerous. Knowing how and when to use our intellect for our benefit, without the interference of emotions, is another. Yet emotional intelligence, the ability to choose what is difficult and uncomfortable but is good for us, is also necessary for positive change. We live in times where information is widely available. It's possible that the combination of too much information and ease of accessibility creates educated, powerless people who know everything but do nothing.

The Happy Body program will require you to do things you may not like at first: eat the right amount of food, eat healthier foods, follow the same exercise routine to measure your progress, force yourself to relax for five minutes. If you do all of this, you will get stronger, healthier and more alive; this is how you build a new past. After one year, when you look back on your improvement you'll see the positive past you've created. And now, when you look into the future, you have the energy and strength for anything you want to achieve, a second chance at life.

In the Happy Body Program you voluntarily trap yourself with a new set of principles, to develop new habits with a desired outcome. We as coaches took responsibility for the formula, the numbers and the science behind it. So we can say that anyone can achieve a happy body, no matter your financial status, country of residence, religion, or culture.

Willpower

The clearest definition of willpower is a drive from within to achieve goals. The word is a combination of two other words: will and power. So we must have a will or desire to pursue a certain goal, and the power to achieve it. The will is an acceptance of what we need to do. If we do not accept that we need to quit smoking because it can cause cancer, for instance, then no matter how much power we have, we will not quit smoking. Aniela's father was diabetic, and when one of his legs was amputated, his doctor told him to stop eating chicken skin. Her father simply responded, "Life without chicken skin is not worth living." He died the following year. He simply did not agree to what could save his life. Yet he still had energy—he was only sixty-seven and very strong. He probably could have lived another thirty years.

On the other hand, we have Jack, who faced prostate removal after his doctors found nodules and a test of his PSA showed 9.5. But Jack would do anything to live, and he knew that if he had a problem with his prostate there could be other issues showing up soon. He asked me what he should do. I said, "Let's try a new diet for six months and see. If it helps, then we will continue, and if not, then you will need surgery. Jack wanted to live, so he agreed to drink juice made from mostly vegetables with added fruits as a sweetener three times a day, eat oatmeal and use only flaxseed oil. After six months his PSA dropped to 2.6. His was doctor was shocked. "What did you do?" he asked. Jack told him. The doctor said, "Wow, just by drinking juice?" When examining Jack, he found that the nodules were not as hard, so he agreed to postpone the surgery another half year. When Jack returned after six months, his PSA was 0.1. "Unbelievable," his doctor said. And when he tested his prostate, there were no nodules left. His prostate was smooth and small. His doctor said that he could go home and they would monitor his PSA every year. After 5 years, Jack's PSA is still in the zeroes, and he never returned to his original diet.

These are illustrations of two people with two different wills. One has a will to live and the other to die. So the will is important, but what about power? Power is the energy that is needed to sustain the will. For example, everyone who is overweight wants to lose pounds, but only those who have power to maintain a different diet can achieve it. And of course there is the main question: what to do after achieving weight loss. Usually when people lose weight they return to their previous way of eating and, as a result, they regain the weight back with a bonus. So even if you have the power to maintain a different lifestyle until you achieve your goal, you may not have any power left to sustain this different lifestyle, and you relapse. The good news is that power is trainable. Its components are intelligence and self-control. Once you learn why you need to change, why when we age we need to work twice as hard to achieve the same results we had when we were young, why we need to do only strength-building exercises, you will tap into the power that will motivate and inspire you to stay healthy forever.

The Happy Body teaches self-awareness by telling someone why they should be a certain weight; which exercises and food choices increase aging and which slow it down; why becoming more youthful is possible; what is the reserve of power at a certain age; and so on. Once a person knows all of this, it is easier for them to wake up the power from within and say I Got This! The Happy Body is a lifestyle, which means it is both a journey and a process. Once goals are established, a plan is created and you have the opportunity to develop all the necessary character traits to achieve and sustain The Happy Body lifestyle. It is like becoming a gymnast: At the beginning the athlete develops a love for the sport, then she becomes patient enough to train for hours a day, and then she learns how to behave when she doesn't win, and she learns to be graceful while facing injuries—everything a person would need to pursue any business endeavor.

Willpower is a wonderful force. It helps us study to become professional. It helps us win and it helps us create. Without it there would be no progress and no evolution. It took a lot of willpower to stop colonial slavery and the Holocaust, so the next time you need some willpower, think about all the people who made our planet a better place. Think about yourself and choose between immediate gratification to satisfy a short-term goal and delayed gratification to achieve the long-term ones.

WHO CANNOT?

Every night when I wake up
I walk to the kitchen.
And every morning
there is still food on my face.
How can I stop myself?

His coach thought for a moment and then told him.
Think about all those people
who stopped themselves
from owning and killing and having fun
because they finally saw
how others suffered.
Without them we would still have slaves,
the Holocaust, and a world just for men.
Becoming a man like that
is your only chance
because there is no one else to force you.

Don't you expect too much from me?
Do you really believe I can be a man like that?

Who cannot?

CHAPTER 8

Responsibility

We are made wise not by the recollection of our past, but by the responsibility for our future.

—George Bernard Shaw

Physical Spirituality

How significant is our birth?

"Each of you is a miracle," my mother used to say to me and my siblings. These words were always echoing in my mind, despite what I was going through, reassuring me how truly miraculous our existence is. Even today, I still contemplate the randomness of even being born at all. We are born into a physical form to experience the physical world around us: the best and the worst, the pain and the pleasure, the beautiful and the ugly.

As we grow up healthy, we take in all that's around us with great interest. Part of us is curious to know more about ourselves from other, outside perspectives. We search for clues to the mysterious, undiscovered parts of ourselves, seeking unusual or surprising qualities beyond the obvious, something that only others can see. That is why horoscopes, tarot cards, psychic and palm readings are so popular. The science of astrology focuses on the position of the sun, moon and stars at the moment of one's birth, attempting to explain future destiny, character, even our personality, talents, and state of health. It's called prediction, and we're encouraged to have "faith" in it.

For thousands of years, people all over the world have considered birthdays special. In pagan times it was believed that on a birthday a person could be helped by good spirits or hurt by evil ones; friends and relatives would gather to support the celebrant. Consequently, more and more people attached certain magic powers to their actual birth date. Today we may wear a necklace or ring with our birthstone, sing special songs, or engage in rituals like bathing and head shaving, depending on the culture, to honor our arrival.

Who doesn't like to celebrate birthdays? Children absolutely love them. Getting together with family and friends and enjoying all the festivities of the occasion like getting presents, blowing out candles and making secret wishes. And of course, eating cake. For one day we are the center of attention—we shine, and it is all about us. Somewhere along the way though, many of us start dreading our birthdays.

Of course there are those who believe that the day of one's birth is not that important, that it merely marks the beginning of our life's journey. To them, what we do with our life is what's important, not how or where we begin. But as we get older it's only natural to reflect as we pass these annual milestones, and that's what Tina did. She came to see us right after she celebrated her 50th.

There are two prime motivations that steer us as we move through life: love and fear. This time Tina was definitely coming from a place of fear. Contacting us was not a random decision. Recently she saw her friend after THB transformation and she was inspired. Tina represented a typical 50-year-old woman: roughly fifty pounds overweight, with pain in her lower back, knees, neck, and shoulder. She felt that this kind of pain and decline were normal for her age, and she shared that she even felt better after seeing high school friends at reunions looking much worse then she did. When we talked, it emerged that her biggest complaints were a lack of energy and general weakness. It seemed at first that she had resigned herself to the aging process.

Yet, Tom and Tina were friends and she knew about his struggles with weight and the resulting physical problems. After not seeing him for about a year, she'd run into him at a party. The room was crowded, but she had spotted a good-looking man smiling at her. She looked over her shoulder to see if there was someone else standing next to her. No, he was looking her. Why me? she'd thought. She felt old, fat and ugly, and even a little embarrassed. She wanted to become invisible. Then suddenly she recognized that the man smiling at her was Tom. The change was impressive; he was a much younger, fitter, and happier version of himself. When Tina asked him how he'd transformed himself, he told her about THB program.

What you practice you become, and this is a hard truth to accept, because it takes responsibility to admit that what we've practiced hasn't brought the results we've wanted. In Tom's case, it was not a lack of effort or laziness that brought poor results from the other programs he tried. And he had tried many: Pilates, yoga, boot camp, all kinds of diets—to no avail. He needed the right tools to get healthy and fit. Just like Tina, he was inspired by one of his friends who had transformed his body with THB program. Tom came from a mindset that "seeing is believing," and he trusted that if his friend was able to do it, then so could he.

"Be careful what you are falling in love with, because it will become your habit," says Dr. Daniel Amen in The Brain in Love. To insure that we live the life that we desire, we need to examine the nature of our physical activity. For example, yoga emphasizes flexibility and focus, and that's what you will be getting if you practice it. Lifting heavier weights will help you to become stronger. Doing sprints will make you faster, and so on.

And so Tina's practice toward bettering her body began. Her progress with weight loss and general physical improvement continued for about three months. She lost about 25 pounds, was lifting heavier weights, and with increased flexibility came less pain. All the changes made her feel really good. Then there were a few weeks when she would come and the scale would show the same weight she had been the previous week. I tried to assure her that it's normal to first learn how to maintain a new weight before dropping more pounds and encouraged her to focus on other aspects of THB standards. Yet soon weeks were passing while her weight stayed the same and her frustration was driving her to tears. She remarked that maybe THB standards for body weight were not realistic at her age. And with her lifestyle of travel and entertaining she wondered if this was as healthy and fit as she would ever be. And....the list was growing longer and more sophisticated each time. Her excuses were piling up like a collection of snowflakes, building a snowman in her mind, ensuring that she wouldn't move toward a different solution to achieve what she really wanted in the first place.

Is it enough to believe we are spiritual?

I think we all have heard this story, at one time or another. In short, it all started with an apple in paradise.

God created the tree of knowledge, of good and evil, and told man and woman not to eat the fruit. The snake's offer of an apple was our first temptation and we failed to resist it.

There is also the old proverb that "one apple a day will keep the doctor away." What do both of these old stories have in common? Fail the temptation of eating just one apple too many a day and you will end up gaining ten pounds a year. Since our metabolic rate decreases as we age, we need to eat the right amount so we don't gain fat with every passing year. How do you resist the temptation of eating more than you need, then? How do you know how much is enough?

This is only an issue for people who live in a country like the United States, those who have accumulated enough resources not to worry about hunger. Never before in history have we faced a problem of abundance; it was always a question of survival and not enough. Only when you have excess are you challenged to learn control. Have you ever wondered if survival was an issue when Adam and Eve picked that apple? Well, maybe or maybe not. They were in paradise after all. If not, we have the situation we are in now, in contemporary times, when we are not hungry and still we eat. And we just don't eat, we eat far more than we need to. Food can provide entertainment and comfort, but it turns into our enemy when we are out of control. We have created a hell when we misuse the food meant to nurture and nourish our body so we can function at our best and live a happy, productive life.

When we moved to our new home in Woodside, one of the most appealing elements of our backyard was the oak trees: the lush European, blue, and California oaks. We named the one that hovered over our little house "Grandpa Oak." But one day we noticed that there was a lot of wood dust littering the ground. To determine its source, we called in a tree expert. After examining Grandpa Oak he told us that it was infested with bugs; there was nothing we could do. The tree was dying. Our daughter Natalie was the most pained to hear the news. After she watched the tree branches being sawed off, the trunk cut and removed, she painted a picture. It showed a tree trunk and what looked like crosses falling from the tree. It was obvious that our daughter was grieving its death. To turn the situation around we looked for positive aspects; for instance, Jerzy pointed out how much more space and sunlight we would have without the tree, which was true. Then I got the idea to name the spot Natalie's Island and gave her the freedom to plant anything she wanted. My daughter got very excited about it. We went to the nearby orchard and bought a small flowering plum tree that we planted in the center. In spring it blooms with pink and white flowers and its leaves are shiny, dark red. Then she planted some herbs and seeds. The spot became a colorful and happy place – a feast for the eyes as well as a resource for birds and bees.

The following year we were preparing the soil for planting and I noticed that Natalie would only work in the corner that we'd weeded together. I wasn't sure why she was avoiding the rest of the space, so I asked her. She admitted that when the plants were so small she was not able to distinguish a weed from a flower, so she didn't want to make a mistake and uproot a flower.

A thought came to me. I saw the whole situation as a parallel to how we behave in life. When we are not sure about things, we are afraid to try; we only stay where is feels safe because we want to stick with what we know. Or we act and make a lot of mistakes; at random we will pull weeds as well as flowers, because they are all green. What I needed to do was slow down and teach her how to recognize weeds and flowers in all their varieties. The same goes with life: we often need someone to show us the better way. When it comes to our lifestyle, we are creatures of habits that grow as we grow. And unfortunately they might actually be like weeds, spreading into our life unwanted when we don't know how to stop or get rid of them.

A cabbage a day?

What about changing the saying from one apple a day to one cabbage a day, especially for those who are already suffering because they are overweight or not healthy? There is a lot of research that cruciferous vegetables help with cancer, so why not to eat more cabbage, cauliflower, broccoli and other vegetables from the root family?

Jerzy is a typical cabbage and potato guy. He used to be meat, potato and cabbage. With time we established a weekly rhythm of eating vegetarian dishes on weekdays, and then a piece of fish or small steak on weekends, if we feel like it. Simplicity and efficiency are very important to Jerzy, so he always looks for the logic in whatever he does. The older he gets the more precisely he pinpoints what does and doesn't work. He despises any kind of waste. When you are young you can waste time and energy; the body is forgiving and it's capable of restoring itself. Sometimes we are just simply lucky. As we get older this latitude slips away, and it's harder to create the kind of body and lifestyle that are good for us.

Jerzy also loves fruit. Jokingly I call him 'my gorilla,' because he is able to eat any fruit in enormous amounts— it's possible for him to consume ten bananas or twenty apples in one sitting. But as we age, that kind of indulgence leads only to weight gain, plus feeling yucky with all the sugar rushes and then the energy dips. But there is something else that we have to look into and question: Is what I'm doing working? And am I achieving what I want? If not, we need to transition ourselves to a different solution.

One of our clients told us that she had been working out for twenty years. Every morning she would meet her girlfriends at the gym, and together they would do the StairMaster while eating muffins. The rationale? They were "carbo-loading" to have more energy to exercise. Our client ended up with a muffin top around her hips. And yet many people work hard in the gym simply to give themselves "permission" to eat more at dinner or a party.

Is it wise to abuse both body and natural resources, just because we want to eat more? What's interesting and obvious to me is that animals in the wild would not survive long if they overate; they would be easy targets for predators. An overfed, sleepy animal is vulnerable. Wild animals' strong, internal survival instinct tells them not to eat more then they need. The sad truth is that many pets lose that innate sense because humans provide food and care for them, eliminating any struggle for survival. Their natural instinct isn't needed, so it becomes dormant. There is a natural satisfaction that comes from doing and achieving. Even animals in captivity prefer to practice their instinctual skills instead of simply being handed food.

We've been pet lovers for many years. There are always animals in our home, ranging from dogs and cats to birds, rabbits, and hamsters. I call our parakeets the soul of the house. Their presence is keenly felt. If the fit is right, birds bond together in a way that resembles a human relationship. They are chirpy and playful, and they groom each other. Once I commented to Jerzy how our birds don't gain weight; they stay healthy for years. Some have lived past the age of twelve. We provide them with different toys for stimulation, along with water and seeds in bowls, but also seeds they have to pick from a branch. They enjoy working with the branch first. They find it rewarding and the satisfaction is visible—they are chirpy and energetically hopping around the cage.

Without a challenge, do we humans lose our instinctual sense too? How do we stay truthful to this feeling so we don't just drift in life? Maybe it is necessary to create, superficially, a state of survival to awaken our own inner fire. As professionals we strive to have better skills, to be better in communication, planning, efficiency, and overseeing progress. It is satisfying to be needed, to be asked for our expertise and informed opinion. This is the edge where some of us strive to keep up with the contemporary world, to attune to what's needed now. Waste in its many forms is one of the struggles most people face all their lives.

And so I had to address the issue of how much food was really enough with Tina. I told her to write in her food journal, again. I asked questions about her daily habits. She started her day early before her family was up, and the first thing she would do was pray. Then she would brew some coffee, have a cup, and do THB exercise routine. Her schedule was busy at work, so she would only have a snack and a light lunch in the form of salad with some protein like chicken or shrimp. By the time she was home, sometimes after being stuck in traffic for more than an hour, she would feel very tired. In spite of this she would cook for her family and, by the time dinner was ready, she would be famished. Usually she would overeat, and at the end she would look for something sweet to treat herself, a desert, even though she knew she'd eaten more than enough. It seemed that she just couldn't stop herself. It's like watching myself doing it and knowing it's wrong, but still doing it anyway. This was how she described the situation. Then I asked her a question.

"Do you consider yourself a spiritual person?"

"Yes!" she said without any hesitation. Her voice sounded very strong.

I waited a little before I asked her the next question.

"So, do you think a spiritual person would ever eat more than needed?"

At this her facial expression changed. There was definitely an emotional war going on inside her, but as hard as the question was, I didn't help or ease her discomfort in answering it. I waited. After a period of uncomfortable silence, she stood up and headed toward the door. She left without saying goodbye.

Afterwards I talked to Jerzy and said that maybe it's too hard for anyone who considers herself spiritual to admit that overeating is not a spiritual practice. I hoped that Tina would take time to think about it, but felt there was only a slim chance that she would return. But despite my predictions, next week she was back. With renewed understanding she recommitted to pursuing the journey of what at first was all about losing weight, but had transformed into something else. She emphasized that now the pursuit was about truly becoming the person she always wanted to be: someone who follows spiritual principles. Her practice meant not only believing in these principles, but also manifesting them in the physical realm.

Over the years, as I was learning about myself, I observed how certain situations triggered undesirable reactions. I saw a strong connection between unconscious emotions and my behavior—which is not surprising—but it led me to dig deeper, to catch these moments so I don't succumb to the same negative outcomes.

I also became observant and sensitive to the behaviors of others around me, and the patterns that we keep repeating, if triggered. Kind of like Maslow's dogs. The good news is that you can teach an old dog a new trick. It just takes an understanding, willingness, and a conscious way of acting to undo the damages.

Who is a spiritual person?

Would you call someone who has an ethical compass a spiritual person? So, what is the difference between being religious and being spiritual? Can you be spiritual but not religious? Yes, you can certainly have high ethical standards and integrity without believing in God or following a structured organization like a church. Can you be religious but not spiritual? Can you be both, religious and spiritual?

All religious practices have a central focus: belief in a higher power. All spiritual teachings are focused on principles and morals meant to humble ourselves, to get rid of ego and self-centeredness, to love and care for another as we would for ourselves, to be mindful about the resources of our planet and avoid abusing it.

After these reflections, a question stirred in me and I needed the answer. Why would I or anyone else overeat if we cared about the planet, clean water and air, about animals not being abused, about others who are hungry? Why would we raise money to build wells for people who lack fresh, clean water, why would we recycle plastic, glass and paper? The simple answer is because we care about not abusing resources, and when do abuse them, we suffer emotionally. So why not to align with what is right to do and just do it?

Well, the answer is not so simple. Why do we have priests, gurus, and even medical doctors who are overweight? Did we forget something essential about the teachings, or has teaching spirituality become a job, where followers are the clients or patients? That would mean that spirituality has just become a business like any other, like selling coffee and donuts or car parts. The only difference is that if you go to the donut shop, you know what you're getting. A business that thrives because it is based on misguided, uneducated, or most often just regular people seeking meaning and purpose in life is questionable if we don't see the importance of role modeling as guidance.

Our problems in life start early on; they begin with habits that are intertwined in our lives—daily routines such as mealtimes, bed times, exercise and hygiene. That's not to say that family traditions like birthdays, anniversaries, reunions, and holiday celebrations don't offer a valuable sense of continuity and grounding. A surplus of rituals or the lack of them illuminates many things about who we are as people, the uniqueness in how we interweave the cultural and the personal patterns of living life. Rituals become our habits, and as we deepen our practice they become so familiar that they become our second nature.

The strongest habits are the slowest to die

It was great to see Tina moving forward, growing. We all know that old habits are hard to change, but it's possible, and she was proving that. A few months later she had another transition that led to drastic shifts in her life. Her last hurdle was alcohol, which was a big part of her lifestyle. She was a self-described "social beast," going out often, traveling, and entertaining at home frequently. Tina believed that having a little vino after a tiring day was okay. This is where she would fail herself—casually opening a bottle of wine to relax, and sipping it while making dinner for her family. Oftentimes at the end of the evening she would be surprised to find that the bottle was empty.

I asked her if she could not drink wine for a week, and she agreed. At the next session her weight had dropped. Then I asked her if she could stop drinking for a month, and she said yes. Great! Her weight was dropping, her eyes were clear and sharp, her face was less puffy and her stomach was flatter. When the month passed she had lost additional pounds, which made her happy. But then her weight started to creep back up. The reason was obvious—she had started drinking alcohol again. My job was to make her aware of what caused the weight gain, to find solutions, but she was the one who needed to cope with it. Her job required dining out: fancy dinner meetings and lunches with coworkers or clients were part of her routine. When she started complaining that there was no way to adjust her eating out, I simply told her to follow the eating schedule and narrow down her choices, as well as choose between having a meal and no wine or half of the meal and a glass of wine. If she wanted to lose weight she had to adjust to what she needed to do, finding a way through instead of complaining.

Then one day she arrived very disturbed, and announced that she would not drink alcohol for the rest of her life. It was an extreme decision, so I asked her why. She told me that the previous weekend, after dinner, she and her husband had sat with couple of friends in their Jacuzzi to relax. Then she woke up, not remembering how their evening had ended or how she had gotten into bed. She was alone, and as she sat up she realized that she was all bloody. Blood was everywhere—on her sheets, her clothes, and on the carpet. She panicked, coming to the point where she imagined she might have killed someone. Terrified, she followed the blood traces that led back to the Jacuzzi. It was empty, but there was blood everywhere. Finally, she realized that the blood was hers. She had gravely injured herself coming out of the water, and hadn't even realized it. Her husband had left for a business trip, and her kids were not at home, so she was all alone. The realization that she could have bled to death shook her up so badly that she decided to stop drinking altogether.

The reasons we drink alcohol are basically the same—to relax and let our defenses down so we can cope better with our stressful, overscheduled days that trigger tension and overanalyzing. If only we knew the perfect amount to drink (and some people do), the practice would be medicinal and beneficial. Some nations, like France, Greece, and Spain, have cultivated a lifestyle that introduces alcohol early. Are these citizens happier and more relaxed? Did they learn how to drink so it doesn't interfere with daily life? I have no answer because I haven't lived in these places. I know one thing, though—if you cannot control something like alcohol, and it controls you, you should either have a strong guideline of how much you're going to have (like one drink) and when and with whom, or not touch it at all. Drinking alone is not an option, because, in the end, it's a social activity.

Do we have to be forced to be good?

So how do we change our relationship with food?

There will always be a force for change. If we would like to change from one who is tempted and reacts to the temptation to one who chooses to stop, there will either be a force from outside, usually in a form of punishment, or a force from within, generating the voice of a person who is aware of how much is enough. All this is not as simple as it seems, however. That's why we need help.

Outside force is the only thing that prompts some of us to stop harmful activities, especially when extreme warnings come to us as they did to Tina. Either we get a message that we are ill, or our spouse is leaving us, or we are about to lose our house, or job—then we start acting on that threat. It's difficult to be proactive or motivate yourself. The wise thing to do would be to choose to start acting before things get bad, not wait and be forced to.

Second Chances – Rebirth

One day, we received news that our friends were getting a divorce after many years together. They had two pre-teen children, and as much as it was painful, Jane made a difficult decision to leave for the good of her children. She had tried to "fix" her marriage, to no avail. Her husband was not responsive to the changes she was making, like eating healthily, exercising, and taking time for relaxation. Their old lifestyle was "spontaneous," as they'd described it themselves when they'd first met, but as time passed Jane realized it was more accurately just chaotic. They were not getting any younger and she had started to worry about their future and the habits they were instilling in their children.

Her husband's behavior was the most problematic. The family ate a typical American diet consisting of pancakes, bacon and eggs, and cereal for breakfast, then pizza, pasta, and hot dogs or hamburgers with french fries, all washed down with soft drinks, for lunch and dinner. Their daughter was overweight and their son was addicted to sugar. As a mother and a woman, Jane knew she needed to help her daughter control her weight before it became an even bigger problem. She started making smoothies and soups, batches of healthy bars, and salads and healthy grains like quinoa with lean meats for dinner. In spite of her efforts, her husband still would bring home junk food like white bread, frozen waffles, cookies, candy, and ice cream. There was no way to convince him to stop, because he considered healthy eating to be deprivation, an attack on his children's "happy" childhood.

But the saddest part of this story concerned their house. As long as we'd known her, Jane had always talked about the changes she planned on making after they'd saved some money. When they decided to separate and sell it, they had to make the house attractive to buyers. She went ahead and made all the changes she'd been dreaming about. When we visited the house just before it went on sale, it was neatly painted with a new roof, with beautifully planted and tended landscaping. All the floors were new; the kitchen appliances and bathrooms had all been upgraded. It was a dream home, but for someone else.

I've seen the same situation occur over and over with changing body image and divorce, where the one who resists the change is left behind. Like Tina, Barb was past fifty. Her children were grown and out of the house. She was overweight, depressed, and she was clinging to her predictable and unfulfilling marriage. The idea of being on her own and her fear of a new, unknown life paralyzed her. Barb was holding on, resisting change until circumstances forced her hand: Her husband moved out, or rather moved on with his life without her. She was lucky that she had good friends who cared about her and helped her transition.

One of her friends suggested that she come see us to start her journey with a positive, healthy lifestyle. Our first sessions were tearful. Change was slow, but she kept coming back consistently. One day after our weekly meeting I found out that she liked numbers, so I recommended a business book entitled The Power of Full Engagement. She read it in a week, and a shift happened in her thinking: she made her body a business and started to take care of it. The idea of achievement and being responsible helped her become reliable, disciplined, and calmer. She became happier when her way of thinking clarified. In a year she turned around her life, dramatically: She lost over sixty pounds, corrected her deteriorated posture, and started working part time. One day she came in and excitedly told me to go outside to see something. A cute, white convertible was parked against the fence. I looked at her; the tired, sluggish woman from months before was all but gone. Instead, standing before me was a very attractive, confident woman dressed in sports clothes with her hair neatly pulled back in a ponytail, her face beaming with pride and joy. She did it all by herself.

Putting Things Together – Critical Thinking

One spring we went to Calistoga for a weekend getaway, just the three of us. It was Jerzy's wonderful idea to book a two-night stay in an inexpensive spa hotel close to downtown. We parked our car and didn't return to it until it was time go back home. Calistoga is a lovely, small town with no chain restaurants or fast food places. Situated in a lush, green landscape with old trees and vineyards opening to views of the surrounding mountains, the town draws a low-key crowd. It's not as publicized and touristy as Napa, but instead offers an inviting escape for family gatherings.

After our first night I woke up as usual at 5:45. I knew from the schedule that there was a yoga class at 6, so I whispered to Natalie and she rose and joined me. We loved it, but when I wanted to go again the next morning she told me to take dad, not her. I smiled as she snuggled back into the covers to sleep in.

We took long walks to explore restaurant destinations and found some interesting antique stores, galleries, and cafes with poetry books to read while drinking your tea. I had a massage and the rest of the time we spent swimming or simply reading books and talking. Our daughter told us details about school, her friends, gymnastics, and the science fair that was coming up. One of our conversations turned to the topic of dinosaurs, and Natalie became animated when she told us what she knew about their extinction. In her understanding, the dinosaurs went extinct because they ran out of food. She also told us about a meteor hitting the Earth, and how there was a huge climate change. Curiously we noticed that she talked about the events as if they were unrelated. She didn't put together the cause and the effect, how because of the meteor the climate changed, which resulted in less food for the dinosaurs and their eventual extinction. After we took some time to review all the events, guiding her so she could put the sequence and causes together on her own, she had an epiphany! It was a good lesson about critical thinking, one that we all need from time to time. We need to pause, to think, and to put things together so we become aware of how things work, so we don't feel like life happens to us, but instead we control whatever we can, and own it.

When we think about how much is enough in life, we need to consider the subjects of entertainment, education, and art.

Entertainment vs. Art

I enjoy entertainment, and think there is place for pure fun and amusement. Writing, dancing, and acting can all provide an enjoyable escape, and it doesn't necessarily have to be deep—humor is good too. Being silly and laughing is a great way to relieve stress. Is there such a thing as "good" entertainment? I think there is, and it's fortifying to join in and express appreciation for people's creativity.

In opposition is Jerzy, who doesn't like entertainment. He might tolerate it, but he generally thinks it's a waste of time, money, or both. He stated once that he's allergic to novels, because they all seem to be the same. Or, almost the same. Opera is predictable, and so melodramatic. Simply put, he doesn't like anything that he has seen or heard before; it bores him and puts him into a "mind coma." As for me I love theater, ballet, movies, and reading novels because it relaxes me. It makes me forget just for a moment about problems, or provides a fresh perspective on them from a different angle. It's an antidote to harsh reality. Good entertainment uplifts me or makes me at least think or feel differently than I did before. It helps restore my trust in creativity and the existence of goodness in people, and celebrate this understanding with others.

Jerzy does love visual art, however, along with non-fiction and any skill-oriented pursuit. I do too, but I also feel that there is a lot of "garbage" out there that I wouldn't consider art just because it is wildly different or extreme. Since we used to disagree on the subject of entertainment and it was a big issue in our relationship, years ago we decided that each week one of us would take responsibility for how we spent our weekend. I would search for "good" entertainment or art, and he would do the same for me. And we couldn't complain or critique each other's choice. That was our compromise, and it worked. When choosing, I was thinking about what he would appreciate the most, like physical skill in contemporary ballet or circus performances, or a good, original story in a contemporary play. He would consider what I would enjoy too, so he would find beautiful architectural monuments, parks, or take me to an art show. This way we had variety, unpredictability, and exposure to things we might not have chosen for ourselves, which could be an enriching experience.

When and how much entertainment to include in our lives is very important, so we don't lose ourselves and drift into substitute "entertainment" with food, exercise, or even with relaxation. How we spend our time is often counterintuitive. Today it's necessary to know what is what and keep it in the place where it belongs. To state outright that food should be for nurturing and nourishing our body to restore it and heal it. But we entertain ourselves with unusual recipes from famous chefs, go to seven-course dinners, or sample new foods that companies come up with all the time. There is a time and occasion for such indulgence, just not too often, and if you start succumbing to weight gain and all kinds of conditions like high cholesterol, high blood pressure or diabetes, it's time to go back to basics: keep food simple and don't overeat.

In the realm of fitness, there are thousands of classes that are purely for fun. So take them only if you have time, after you've done some form of physical activity that makes you stronger, more flexible, faster, with improved posture, and doesn't overuse or abuse your joints. And, when it comes to relaxation or stress release, it is simple if you don't overdo the other two—eating and exercise. You don't have to go to special retreats on the other side of the world to discover that a simple walk in nature will bring back the connection with trees, sky, wind and earth. Or people. It is detoxifying and regenerating and doesn't cost much. Life expectancy today is longer then ever: eighty-two years for men, eighty-six for women. Before it was normal to retire and then die within a couple of years; we didn't have to face the results of our lifestyles for decades. Now we need to plan how we are going to live the next half of our life when we are in our fifties, and often undo bad habits and learn more effective ways of living, but it's all worthy and meaningful. I believe that we are all special. As Pierre Teilhard de Chardin said, "We are not human beings having a spiritual experience: we are spiritual beings having a human experience." To seize the opportunity for this precious experience, we would hope to learn the principles of living a good life so we can leave this place better, or at least not worse than we found it.

Enough

The most important word in life is enough. The world's existence depends on this word. There must be enough space between the sun and the earth. Otherwise, we would die of either excessive heat or cold. We constantly bounce between too much and too little. We need to learn the concept of enough every time we approach something new, whether it's riding a bicycle or playing the piano. To stand upright as infants, we have to go through the process of learning to make the necessary adjustments, to avoid falling either forward or backward. As soon as we lose our balance, we sit down, returning to a more stable position.

Only a person who learns how much is enough, who has learned balance, can become a master of their craft. A medical doctor knows how much medicine to prescribe, a musician knows how long or how forcefully to play a note, a businessperson knows exactly how much to invest. Athletic coaches on a daily basis must know what is enough for their athletes. If they train their athletes too hard, they run the risk of exhaustion or injury. If they do not train them hard enough, on the other hand, the athletes will not progress sufficiently to achieve their goals.

The more advanced the craft, the more challenging it is to know how much is enough. The more sophisticated the discipline, the narrower the gap between too much and too little—and the more mastery required on the part of the teacher. A music teacher who does not hear their students' mistakes should refer them to another teacher who is perceptive enough to hear the problems. Balance involves constant adjustment between too much and too little. Without adequate mastery, we suffer the consequences. When it comes to food, for example, if we eat too much, we eventually become obese—while if we eat too little, we eventually starve.

What is enough becomes essential whenever we want to achieve anything. Consider, for example, the case of Mary, who struggled with her weight all her life. Two years ago, at 5'6", she was 150 pounds. At 40 percent body fat, with 60 pounds of fat and 90 pounds of muscle, she wanted to lose weight. Since she did not know how much she should weigh, she did not know how much weight she should lose. Not knowing her ideal weight, she had only her intuition to go by. After she lost 30 pounds, she was still at 35 percent body fat: 42 pounds of fat and 78 pounds of muscle. She felt weak and had lower energy because she ate too little. She therefore began eating more, but since she did not know how much more she should be eating, she ate too much. She slowly regained strength but also gained weight. This scenario repeated itself frequently, making her feel frustrated and disappointed. She began to think of herself as a "loser." Eventually she the lost the willpower to help herself control her desired body weight.

By coincidence, one day, while searching the Internet, she stumbled upon The Happy Body Program and emailed me to help her. I analyzed her situation, so she could understand what happened to her and why. I told her that there was one reason for her fatigue and her inability to maintain her weight. She ran two hours every day on a treadmill, which caused her to lose muscle. In this way, she became skinny, obese, and tired; she was under-muscular and overfat. Her body mass went down from 90 pounds to 78 pounds. Because she lost 12 pounds of muscle, she became weak and unable to sustain her weight.

I told her that she needed to know what her ideal body weight should be, in order to lose weight intelligently and scientifically. At her height, her Ideal Body Weight was supposed to be 122 pounds. Ideally, she should have 13 percent body fat, so her muscle should weigh 106 pounds and her fat, 16 pounds.

Gaining muscle would make her youthful—strong and energetic, but it would take her 16 months to restore her baseline muscle first. Only by building enough strength to stress her existing muscle would she be able to gain muscle weight. Muscle grows because we get stronger, not because we eat more protein.

"Isn't it difficult to grow so much muscle at my age?" Mary asked.

"Aging means muscle atrophy," I said, "The older we are the less muscle we have."

"How can I gain muscle then?" Mary asked.

"First," I said, "you need to stop the exercise that burns your muscle, which would be any endurance activity. Then you need to do only strength-building exercises that promote muscle growth. Muscle grows slowly, so don't try to grow it faster than you can. In the meantime, you should eat enough to lose weight until you reach 122 pounds, then stay with the plan for 16 months and you will build all the muscle you need. Then you will feel as strong as ever. The signs of aging will simply vanish and you will undertake tasks as if you were twenty years old.

The idea of enough must be examined against what we want to achieve. If you want to gain 15 pounds of fat in a year, then one apple a day more than you need would be enough. If you want to lose 15 pounds of fat in a year, then one apple less a day than you need would be also be enough. When we get stronger, our metabolic rate increases, so we need to increase our intake of food to sustain our body weight. But when we age, we get less muscular and weaker; our metabolic rate decreases so we need less food to sustain our ideal weight.

IT FEELS YOU

A Safeway cashier pulled out
a two-liter bottle of diet soda and put
it in front of the apples.

I looked at it and said,
"I didn't buy this."
She smiled and said, "It's okay, it's free."

"I'm sorry," I said, "but I don't want it."
She smiled more sweetly and said,
"But it's free. You can have it."

"The truth is," I said, "I wouldn't
drink it even if I was paid to."

She stopped laughing and said,
"You must be an immigrant."
"No. I'm a true American," I told her.
"A true American?" She smiled.
"Yes," I said, "hard to change from outside."
She took the bottle away and said,
"I don't even remember how that feels."
"That's alright. It feels you."

CHAPTER 9

Mastery

Only one who devotes himself to a cause with his whole strength and soul can be a true master. For this reason mastery demands all of a person.

—Albert Einstein

Are Women a Magic Pill for The Family?

I grew up with nine brothers and was one of the youngest in the family. It was not an easy childhood because, as a girl, I could easily be put down, overrun, or dismissed, if not ignored. Consciously or not, my brothers tried to reduce me to certain feminine roles such as cleaning, washing, and cooking. The things women were supposed to do in the old days–serve men—while men were doing the important things. The older I became the more I tried to stand up to them, rebel, and defend my growing, fragile self. At the same time I tried to figure out who I was without projections from anyone and discover what I was good at. It was not a simple task with so much testosterone in the house. The fact was that no one seemed to be interested in either helping me find my true self or guiding me in my personal growth.

My father was rarely home and, when he was, he was working or resting from work. We were left to cope with problems on our own. I can only guess that my brothers were managing their own lives as well as they could. Many times with my father gone, my oldest brother was filling in for his responsibilities, taking care of the younger kids.

I don't know if they had any long-term plans about their future, aside from every day survival. They seemed to follow the principle that "life will happen, no matter what." There were certain expectations about girls that were projected on generation after generation: when she is ready she will get married, have kids and be taken care of by a man.

On the other hand, my brothers were preparing themselves for the role of caretakers for their future families. If that sounds like the Middle Ages, you should know it is still happening even today in certain environments.

Sadly, I couldn't count on my mother's help, because she herself was overwhelmed with the demands of every day life. Time was passing by, and I saw a kind of resignation and acceptance with her role at home and in life as caretaker. I had to look for help outside my home, through school and other activities like singing and acting.

I think many young girls are dealing with the same issues in spite of the fact that it is 2016. In many ways life is the same and the decisions that girls have to make are not different today than they were for me. The decisions are either made for us, or life just randomly happens to us, shaping a future that we are not always happy with.

The time between girlhood and womanhood passes quickly, and the responsibility that comes with it can devastate and overwhelm many. That's why we either don't have any image of what our lives should be, or we lose sight of who we would like to become. Getting married too young, or starting work too early, instead of pursuing an education, cuts off the opportunity to discover ourselves. It all starts with imagination, and action and reaction after that.

Our daughter, who is twelve, likes to bake. Jerzy and I laugh that there must be baking genes passed on to her since her grandfather was also a baker. In her free time, she gets an IPod or a cookbook and just follows the recipe to make whatever she wants. She learned without any supervision how to make banana bread, pumpkin bread, pumpkin pie, muffins, scones and chocolate chip cookies. They are not only edible but really great tasting.

One thing we observed with her and her friends is the pride they take in creating things from scratch, or, you could also say, from a bunch of random ingredients. I feel strongly that as mothers we need to encourage our children to do things from "scratch" and let them know that it's okay to mess up. Whether it is painting a picture, making a basket, arranging flowers, or baking bread, it's all right not to make something perfect, because there's always next time. It's part of learning. Only with practice do we get better. One day I picked Natalie up from gymnastics. As she settled in she said, "I wish I had a clone."

I was curious why she said this.

"Why would you want to have a clone?"

"Because I would ask the clone to do gymnastics for me, or homework, or other things."

I thought this was worth exploring with her to open up her imagination.

"So Natalie, let's imagine that you have a clone and you tell the clone to do all the things that are required of you. The clone would do everything you ask or wish for. Then, what do you think would happen to you? The clone would be the doer. She would do baby giants in gymnastics, learn perfect Spanish, and write wonderful essays for English class. But you wouldn't. How would you feel, staying the same, watching your clone getting better at things?" She was listening, processing what I was saying so I kept going.

"Do you remember how if you didn't practice piano for a while, you kind of forgot how to play, and you needed to practice just to get back to where you left off? Do you think the same would happen with all the other things you do?"

"Well maybe it's not such a good idea after all. It looked that way at first, but I see what you're saying—practice makes us better."

"Yes. Look at gymnastics. Someone would have to spend the same or even more time to catch up to your skill level. But you're not standing still; you keep practicing and moving forward, so catching up to you is really impossible. Do you see?"

The child's mind, the wishful thinker…how many of us get stuck in this mind and never overcome challenges to upgrade our lives and ourselves. We are waiting for somebody to do it for us, expecting that somehow we will get what we want or where we want to be without our conscious effort.

When I met Jerzy, he was a competitive athlete and a great student and I had a lot of admiration for him. We enjoyed our conversations, walking for hours around our hometown. But after a while and a few hot discussions, I decided that he had an even bigger ego than all my brothers put together. So we split. I felt that I didn't need another man telling me how to think, feel, or what to do. We didn't see each other for over a year. I dated someone else and so did he. But as our friends were telling us, we had a natural propensity for each other, and we ended up getting back and eventually getting married.

Later, I understood that I needed to stay with my own way of thinking and feeling and that only I had the power to persuade him if he was wrong, or misunderstood something. And instead of getting offended and closing up through withdrawal, I needed to listen and reflect. That has been one of my challenges in life, to keep talking until there is mutual understanding. This didn't happen easily, and it still doesn't, because it shouldn't.

There were times when I would get offended and barricade myself in a room. Jerzy would bang on the door, trying to get me to come out to talk until we understood each other's point of view. We don't have to agree, necessarily, but with time we've learned to respect our differences in thinking. That's the spice of a relationship that evolves: it helps both partners to grow up, grow out of habitual thinking, and to accept the challenge of seeing things in different ways.

One day I had a conversation with Jerzy about women and their role in the world. It started as a simple exchange of ideas about how women were viewed throughout history and what were society's expectations of them. We both saw how women are naturally physical and emotional nurturers, healers, farmers, chefs, and artists... the list can go on and on. I pointed out the difference between men and women, who are peaceful warriors. Women are not focused on killing, plundering, and robbing, but on creating a better society by establishing rules and laws. Coexistence and being together is very important to them. We might not like each other but our survival as a society is a high priority. (Of course there are exceptions, possibly created by the existence of men and the competiveness that surrounds them. For instance, in the book Women's Inhumanity To Other Women, the author explores female relationships in different cultures, and how women can undermine and exclude each other.) Over the years, Jerzy has expressed the opinion that the world would be a better place if women ran it.

If you watch interactions among small children, you can see nature at its best and worst. Often at the playground, I've seen groups of girls making cupcakes, dressing up dolls, and playing house, whereas boys roughhouse or play destructive games where they have to smash or crush something. The boys' focus is on the physical power struggle, and the girls' is on the emotional.

When do the projections on women actually start? Women are assigned roles that are passed on from one generation to another like an Olympic torch. This becomes habitual thinking. Only when parents actually "grow up" do shifts happen in the family. Change is possible.

In our discussion, Jerzy pointed out how much we depend on women to create a certain mood at home so the family feels peaceful and happy. Well, at first I got very defensive. I accused him of not feeling responsible for what, in my mind, was our life together. I felt as if he was pointing a finger at me, expecting me to fix things if they were not right.

Our passionate discussions always produce some kind of insight and solution to the problem we are coping with. His experience and memory of his own mother was: "When my mother was happy, not only were we happy at home, but the whole street we lived on was happy.

If she was not happy, it felt like there were dark clouds gathering above our heads, even when the sun was out."

Taking Charge

I thought about what Jerzy said for some time, about my own mother and the mothers of my friends, and it was an eye-opening exploration. When I was growing up, I watched my mother struggling all the time to keep our family above water. Her days were filled with food shopping, the preparation of meals, sewing or repairing clothes, cleaning, and doing laundry. Even though my mother stayed at home, caring for eleven kids can be more than a full-time job.

I remember one summer when I was eleven years old and my family was experiencing financial difficulties. There was no hope of money coming in, so my mother came up with a way to help the family. She decided that one of my older brothers would take us in his truck to the other side of Poland where my aunt had a farm. We harvested strawberries, picked bugs off of potatoes, stacked hay, and milked cows, along with other farm work. It was different and fun for us city slickers to learn all these new tasks we'd never done before.

Scarcity taught my mother how to become an alchemist in the kitchen. She would come up with so many different ideas of what to cook so we could enjoy a variety of dishes created from the cheapest, simplest, most basic ingredients. She was never intimidated in any kitchen because she always found a way to make things from whatever was available.

Many of our clients, when they come to us for the first time, are already aware that they cannot maintain the same eating habits. But they are confused about what to eat, how much to eat, when to eat, and what kinds of foods are best for them. Their idea of cooking is more about deciding where to order take-out than looking into kitchen cupboards to create something from scratch. Food preparation, for them, is pulling out a box of pasta or a cake mix and following the directions. This kind of "cooking" is less expensive than going to restaurants or a bakery, but those products are full of preservatives, colorings, and emulsifiers that, over time, will have an ill effect on the body.

Too many women have lost that sense of magic in the kitchen. Did it begin when women started to work while raising a family? When one paycheck was not enough for the family to pay the bills? Did it come with a lifestyle of too much affluence? Gadgets for the kitchen, gadgets in the living room, gadgets and more gadgets, whether we need them or not. Then, to supposedly help women, the food industry introduced pre-packaged foods that took less time, but at the expense of the nutritional value of real foods. It was a tradeoff that sacrificed health. Women work, earn money, and then spend it on pre-packaged foods that make their families unhealthy. When the medical bills start showing up, the quality of life goes down. It is a vicious circle that it is hard to break, because it becomes an established pattern in a culture that's trying to adapt to overwork.

So are women the magic pill for the family? What is the solution to keep our families well? Where can we look for it? Perhaps we need to explore some other possibilities.

I work with many therapists, so one day, just out of curiosity, I asked one of them about the primary emotion that drives people these days. I was surprised when, without any hesitation, she suggested that anxiety was the major cause of people's problems. And women tend to have more anxieties and ruminate on them more than men do.

Solving Problems

Women and men solve problems differently, and my family is a good example. We love animals, and so our home has always been a safe haven for cats, dogs, birds, hamsters, and fish. Once we were fortunate to have a bunny. All these animals came into our life, sometimes unexpectedly.

There was the time when we were coming out of the movies and found an injured dove sitting near the wall of the entrance. Everyone else passed it by, ignoring it, but of course we couldn't let it suffer. We took it with us and went on a rescue mission.

Another time I found a baby opossum in the middle of the road as I was driving to meet a client at the gym. It must have fallen out of the mother's pouch. Luckily, it was very early Saturday morning so there were not many cars. I picked it up and brought it to the gym. It was so cute we wanted to keep it as a pet, but later, as the woman at the rescue shelter pointed out, California law forbids it, so we had to leave it there.

We sometimes feel like we are magnets for rescuing people and animals, mending broken beings. One day

I saved a lovebird from a cat's mouth. Literally, I took it from her teeth. The bird's skin was a little torn, but not terribly, so the bird didn't bleed to death. We kept it in our living room where it hopped from chair to chair around the dining table. When it got better, it started to climb our curtains, walking on the curtain pole and making a hole in the fabric.

We posted information about it around the neighborhood, but nobody claimed it. After two weeks or so, after it had enlarged the hole in the curtain, chewed all our cookbooks in the kitchen, and shredded some more books from the bookcases, I asked Jerzy to get a cage. Instead he said that he would build one. He went to the garage and used all kinds of stuff we had stored there.

He used branches from our pruned lemon tree for structure. Then he came up with the idea to drill holes and thread plastic wire to create a mesh enclosure so the bird couldn't slip through. And this is where he got stuck for couple of weeks, weaving and threading something he started and intended to finish.

He even made a swing, a climbing ladder and some other toys for its enjoyment. At the end, the cage looked like a wonderful, Hawaiian hut. We brought it along with us wherever we moved, and it was used for our new birds over the years. One day, our daughter noticed a wide hole in the mesh.

"Dad, you have to fix it, otherwise the birds will fly out," she said.

He didn't say anything. He looked around. She was standing next to a tray filled with fruit, and without much thinking, he picked up a banana and stuck it through the mesh, blocking the hole. My daughter and I looked at each other, startled. Then we started laughing so hard we couldn't stop.

If I were trying to solve this problem, I would overthink it. I would explore cages in a pet store, compare prices, maybe even order one from Amazon. Jerzy found an immediate solution.

So, what about stress? First let's explore the topic of stress, which seems to be the number one cause of many health conditions, and, as Jerzy says: "It doesn't exist."

The book Why Zebras Don't Have Ulcers by Robert Sapolsky illustrates how we are different from animals when it comes to stress, or stressful situations. When a lion chases a zebra, it's all about killing to satisfy hunger, while the zebra is motivated by survival in its flight. The race is on, and then the lion either catches the zebra, or stops before long, because otherwise the lion would die of dehydration. So it lies down and rests. Meanwhile, the zebra grazes with the rest of its herd nearby and no one is stressed, and they all go about their business as before the encounter.

An animal's life is simple: either you eat or you are eaten. With humans, things are a bit different. When facing a stressful situation, we act or react, but most of us, if we achieve undesired results, don't stop there. We go over and over in our minds about what happened. We rationalize, analyze, scrutinize and so on, which pumps up our hormones and then leaves us drained. Afterwards we are exhausted and not able to function well for a while. Then slowly we recover, and we might even accept what happened. Until the next stressful situation. Or stress might become chronic, almost second nature, and we might end up flooding ourselves with stress hormones all day long, until we collapse.

When two people experience the same situation and one is stressed out and the other is not, it means only one thing: our attitude is a choice. Women play many roles in life and each of them requires certain skills. We are daughters, sisters, wives, lovers, and workers. So I agree with Jerzy that stress doesn't exist; only challenging situations exist.

Managing

Women often feel overwhelmed because we need to learn how to become better at managing our lives. No matter what, our lives will consist of the same activities, and ¬"time is money." If we either do too much or too little of something, we can overlook essential elements that should be priorities in our lives.

The question is how can you adjust your lifestyle to create a simple and manageable life? Knowing what you want sets you free, and liberates you. If you don't know what you want, you may never stop searching for something indefinable, but if you are lucky you might find a person who will open your eyes to that.

Let's take the practice of Zen Buddhism and devoting yourself to it to pursue simplicity. A Zen lifestyle cannot easily be applied to contemporary existence. The lifestyle of the average woman—if she has the complexities of work, home maintenance, fund raising, tax preparation, and kids' school demands to coordinate—is both complex and overwhelming,

What we can take from Zen is the principle of living simply, living with purpose so that we pursue meaning in life, make sure we feel it's worth living. Recently I read an interesting story about a 103-year-old Japanese doctor. He practiced medicine until retirement, but didn't stop working. "The first sixty years we work for our families and for achieving our goals. Afterwards, we should direct our efforts in favor of the society. I have been working as a volunteer for sixty-five years. I can work for eighteen hours each day of the week to this day. And I enjoy every single minute of it." These are the words of doctor Shigeaki Hinohara. Being useful and needed makes us happy.

Eating healthily is another area where we lose perspective. We obsess about cholesterol and trans fats and what's on the label, so we take supplements and monitor proteins and carbohydrates. But how much does all this information actually help us and how much does it take us away from the simplicity of eating well?

The best approach is to keep it simple, to know exactly what is enough and whether something is essential and benefits our families. Learn to say no when you feel overwhelmed; say yes to things that you are passionate about, that challenge you and help you grow as a person.

Be engaged in making the world around you a better place through your actions. It takes maturity, but what else is there if not the desire to grow up, no matter what your age?

A Different Perspective

Years ago, I saw the movie "Lost in Translation," and I would like to bring attention to the title concept, which I've seen many times in different contexts. Sometimes we can gain in translation, and this is how it happened to us:

We came to United States as political refugees. Even though we had opportunities to stay in other countries, we were determined to begin our new life here, because we believed in the fundamental principles of this country, like freedom, independence, and self-realization, to name just a few. If not here, where else could we find them? This was 1986.

As immigrants we looked at life in the U.S. with fresh eyes (too often with the eyes of ignorance, admiration and above all, enthusiasm). Just like children. In starting a new life, we needed to learn things from the bottom up. Of course we had to grow up fast, and assume the roles of our chronological age in order to function as productive citizens of this country.

This is where our fresh outlook got us to thinking. We get used to things that are already established in our native environments. There is a certain familiarity and comfort with the culture, customs, rituals and so on. As we were "growing up" we learned how things work, why they work, the rules, the laws, and social dynamics. But being new we could make comparisons, see differences, and question established rules and laws.

We discovered great things that we appreciated and things that obviously did not work and needed to be changed. So the question was how to change things that were outdated and didn't work anymore. We learned that change is slow, and requires patience and a strong will.

This is where we see the clear division between people: those who are proactive and adapt, and those who wait until they are forced by circumstances to change.

The United States is a country based on free choice, and there are responsibilities and consequences that come with this. The first months we arrived in California, after making the conscious choice to leave our sponsor in Detroit, we had help from the government in the form of welfare. We both found jobs very quickly, because we intentionally looked for them. The checks kept coming in the mail, so after couple of months we decided to collect them and return to the welfare office. It was a big trip to take at that time; we had an old Chevy with a broken carburetor. But we did, and to our surprise the office clerk told us to keep all the checks and accept the new ones until the end of the year. We simply thanked her and told her about our jobs. We felt that we didn't need help anymore; we could support ourselves and we were aware of others who were more in need. As we were leaving, the woman looked at us as if we were insane.

As new immigrants, we actively participated in making constant changes and devoted our lives to this pursuit. Liberation has to come from inside each person. What we gain in translation is adapting an outworn way of living to the contemporary context.

When we reached a point in our lives where we accumulated enough to start making choices, we needed to take conscious control so we didn't end up wasting or destroying what we'd built.

How do we get to that place where we become too stuck or disgusted with our lives that, instead of making constructive change, we retreat to a place where we become depressed and hopeless? There is no visible line that we cross. One day can bend, or straighten out a life. Destroy or rebuild it. One person can help you to elevate or bury yourself. But we need to discover ourselves first to make a difference in our own lives. There is always a reason, and that takes motivation and inspiration.

My friend Wendy suggested that The Happy Body Program, to her, was like stitching her own parachute. By incorporating THB principles, like having three snacks and two meals spaced every three hours, doing THB exercise routines and practicing relaxation afterwards, she was changing incrementally. Every day she added a little bit so, whereas she might have felt overwhelmed with lifestyle change before, practicing the program now grounds her.

Her old pattern was to exercise frequently when she had a lot of free time, but then she also gave herself permission to overeat. She was just treading water, with no goals and no deep understanding of why she was exercising. On the other hand, when she was busy, she would not make time to exercise or take time to eat and relax. From too much to not enough, this was her staccato pattern of repetition.

There are some things in life that are timeless that don't have to be changed. Just like classical music, or great art created to endure, THB was created in a time of abundance and waste to establish a healthy relationship with the world around us. This new relationship can allow us to focus on more important issues.

We hope that more and more people will learn to make conscious choices about eating just enough, setting a precedent for future generations that leads us away from disastrous overconsumption.

At the time we were not aware that when we created the THB Program we created a "symphony." A smooth, consistent practice pieced together so we might achieve a better quality of life. What we want and what we need can be two different things. If you're constantly distracted by overeating and the pursuit of trivial exercise to compensate, you're focusing on the wrong things. If the right practices become second nature and your body becomes happy, you're free to lead a meaningful life and be ready for anything that comes your way.

Variety

In 1785, British poet William Cowper said: "Variety's the very spice of life, that gives it all its flavor." I imagine he was addressing people who didn't have any variety in their lives, people who ate the same food every day or worked in a factory doing the same thing over and over. These people craved variety. For them it meant a better life. In 1950s America, after a hundred years of craving and dreaming about variety, the population found more affordable products delivered to stores than ever before. Finally people could live a satisfying life.

At the beginning, people could probably recognize which potatoes were best and which farmer grew them. As variety for the consumer increased over time, more products appeared: potato chips, potato pancakes, wedges, fries, tater drums, and many more. When we ate more products, however, we lost the ability to recognize which potato was good. Without this ability, we were unable to choose better quality foods. Today there are hundreds of different brands, so when you go to a store to buy mustard there are 300 jars to choose from. After browsing, you find you like too many of them and you are unable to make a choice. You get dizzy, so you call your wife and she tells you which one to select. If she doesn't know, then you have to choose yourself, so you pick one randomly and bring it home. If you're lucky, you choose one that you like. Yet, since all the products are almost the same, we learned to like the idea of variety rather than a particular product. We can eat any mustard. The final stage of our shift from quality to quantity happens when we like everything and we always pick up a different mustard to try something new. It simply does not matter anymore that one is better than the other, because we lost that ability to know. When it comes to mustard or drinking a different wine, there is no issue, but when it come to eating or exercising, the quest for variety can be a problem. For people who want to achieve any kind of progress variety means trouble.

In the 80s there were personal trainers in gyms whose purpose was to make people stronger or leaner. Trainers understood what was important and created a plan to achieve the goal, and the goal was the same for everyone—getting stronger and leaner meant getting healthier. But people wanted variety, and since they were paying, they pressed their trainers to entertain them with different exercises. A huge variety of exercises were created, and as years passed by trainers forgot that there was any goal in the first place. Entertainment became the goal. People began living a life where "going to the gym" was their main purpose. Every day they took a different class or started a different exercise program.

Today, there is certainly a lot of variety in gyms. There are hundred different classes on offer, the more the better. All classes have the same purpose: to entertain people so they don't feel bored. But of course the instructors cannot say that entertainment is now the whole goal, so they say that the goals are the same as they were 40 years ago: becoming stronger, achieving better posture or becoming leaner, even though most classes cannot deliver these results.

People who take classes say that they are happy, but after years they become more and more disappointed and depressed because they don't lose weight or they don't become stronger or more flexible. They then think that they're aging, and assume that this is why they're getting worse. When they communicate this to their trainers, they agree. So some people believe that an inevitable decline is normal and do nothing. Others know it's not them, but that the system itself is flawed, so they go out and search for something better. The journey is rocky because the whole fitness industry is about entertainment. After losing more years, they discover sports. As soon they start practicing swimming or tango or weightlifting, skill-building and goals become the center of attention. Coaches replace trainers, focus replaces boredom, and quality replaces variety. They are told that what they want is not the primary motivator, what they want to achieve is the primary goal. They are told that like all athletes, they need to follow a plan and break records. Practice the same routine over and over until it's perfect and then they can move on to more a complex routine. Their plans and strategies will now be tested by the achievement of goals. So from now on, nothing is wrong with the sport we practice and everything is wrong with us if we don't get better. No more do we hold the idea that something is wrong with a particular class or a trainer. Now if we don't achieve what we planned, we examine our plans and change them so they are better aligned with achievement.

The Happy Body established six measurable standards and goals to achieve youthful and healthy living. The quality of these standards determines your quality of life, but it is never static. As you master a specific level there is always another that is more challenging ahead of you. This orientation of constant improvement takes root in your brain, and your life and the world become better because of it.

KNOWING

While looking at a billboard picture
of a delicious burger with fries,
John told his wife, No wonder we get fat.
That's why you think we get fat? Mary said,
just because of beautiful pictures?
It's not just a beautiful picture, John said.
I salivate while I look at it.
These food producers should be ashamed.
Ashamed of what?
John's mouth started to twitch.
You know exactly what I'm talking about.
Making our nation obese.
Would you do anything differently
if you were one of them?
Of course! John burst out.
I would help people to eat just enough.
So what would you be, a philanthropist?
It's simply not human to make
people eat more than they need.
Is it human to blame?
Yes. Weakness is human.
So, do we become human
because we are weak?
John kept silent for more than a minute.
Then, how can we resist these masters of seduction?
By knowing what is just enough.

CHAPTER 10

Maturity

Maturity is the ability to think, speak and act your feelings within the bounds of dignity. The measure of your maturity is how spiritual you become during the midst of your frustrations.

—Samuel Ullman

Quick Fix: Gambling with Your Future

I am not the only one in my family who loves to travel. My father was on the move all the time, evidenced by the birthplaces of my siblings, who for the most part, were born in different towns. And there were eleven of us. As I later learned, our father moved from place to place not because he wanted to, but in search of work.

My father was a great baker, passionate about his trade. Baking was something that he knew with his hands as well as his heart. His entire life, he was a baker. Wherever he worked, his expertise and experience always made a positive contribution. His skill, craftsmanship and work ethic consistently earned him the respect and admiration of other bakers.

He was also not an easy man to work with, however, mostly because he had such high standards. He expected the best from himself, as well as from others. Sometimes he took us to whatever bakery he worked at, to help him. He expected us, as his children, to perform better than his workers. Watching us with an eagle eye, he was quick to scold us in front of all the other workers, to the point that we would cry and secretly hate him for humiliating us. We watched him mixing huge, metal bowls of dough that would be transformed into loaves of breads, dinner rolls, pies and all kinds of cookies people would buy in the local bakery shops.

Seeing him at work, there was no doubt about his love of baking. He was always striving to improve established recipes and invent new varieties of products to please and entertain his customers. There were times when he went for an entire week on only one hour of sleep. His hard work brought him a small bakery of his own and a café that my mother managed. With his newly acquired wealth, however, came a new habit that eventually ruined him and brought destruction to our family. This new habit was poker.

A group of wealthy men in town met regularly on weekends to play poker, drink and socialize. This is how my father started spending his free time and his money. At first, he would lose some money then win some back, nothing major. Then one day he placed a very large bet, using his bakery and café as a deposit. He was sure he would win. But poker is a game of chance and this bet proved to be unlucky. After he lost, the family moved to another town and began anew. The situation repeated itself: Father rebuilt the business, gambled and lost it again. After that, he was never again at his prime. He was relegated to working at the bakeries of other people, moving often from town to town in pursuit of greater opportunity.

His newer, less expensive habit became the state-run lotto. He devised elaborate systems, recorded in numerous journals. Although there were some occasional winnings, overall, he lost much more than he ever won. He would even try to borrow money for gambling from his children and on one occasion secretly "borrowed" one of his son's entire savings, without the son's knowledge. Father never came into the fortune that he craved.

I know all this from stories from my older brothers who, to this day, hold grudges against our father. When I was born, my family had already been experiencing poverty for some time. I have only very limited memories of living in a modern, sunny apartment surrounded by a big park. I used to play all day long. I had no knowledge of life with nannies, a family bakery or café—the life that my older siblings had known. The place I called home was in the old part of the town, the pre-war, typical, three-story German-built apartment that was falling apart, with no government money to repair or remodel it. This is where I grew up and spent most of my early life. The toilets we had access to were located off the stairways between the different levels and shared with the neighbors. The apartments were heated by coal furnaces. Water leaked in from the roof and the window frames were falling out of the walls. The life I knew was one of doing without, going hungry, feelings of cold and despair, watching my mother trying to keep the family alive and together.

When I was a teenager and my father was a tired middle-aged man, I asked him why he gambled so much and took such great risks. He explained his thinking process as one of good intentions. He was young and wanted to bring financial freedom to his growing family. His plan was to work hard and accumulate money. He wanted to speed up the process of accumulation through gambling. That was the only way he could think of to move forward more quickly with his plans.

Poker should rightfully be a form of entertainment only. But my father naively played with professionals, with whom he was no match and who took advantage of him. He ceded his power to these men through his obsession with gambling. The saddest realization for me was that my father was blind to the real wealth that he possessed, the wealth that came from his own hard work. He failed to see that his self-destructive behavior only made other people wealthy, depriving his family of security and any future. The quick fixes he tried were doomed to fail and in fact, did fail. The quick-fix approach becomes a way of living at the expense of legitimate long-term solutions. So it is with gambling, drinking, shopping and even exercising.

It is perhaps more difficult in some ways to stay with one craft, enhancing one's level of skill and deepening one's knowledge, but this approach is also the most rewarding. Whether playing a musical instrument, writing poetry, becoming a swimmer or a businessman — it all requires commitment. Many hours of practice are needed in order to get better, to achieve a high level of mastery. The same principle applies when it comes to our health and fitness. Just reading books or information on the Internet will not make you a master of any craft, although some of the knowledge derived in this fashion will be helpful. Rather, it is through practice and the continuous feedback you receive as a result of this practice that you will achieve the desired results.

When I started working as a personal trainer in Los Angeles almost thirty years ago, part of my job was to teach people how to use the gym equipment. I also taught them the purpose of each exercise and created programs to meet the specific needs of the individual. After a while, I noticed that what I was doing was in effect coming up with quick fixes for my clients. So when they had fat thighs, I asked them to do more exercises for their legs. If they had "love handles," I would design a program to specifically target this area and so on. After one thing was fixed, another came into view. People were coming and going and results were random, often leaving me with feelings of frustration and dissatisfaction. I am sure that many of my clients felt the same way, not finding a lasting solution to their problems.

I had two things to hold onto in life: weightlifting and poetry, with a clear roadmap as to what I needed to do in order to achieve clear goals. I needed to learn what was effective and what made me a better craftswoman. Weightlifting competitions taught me how to be efficient physically. Earning an MFA in creative writing equipped me with tools to write better.

In athletics, all athletes have the same thing in mind: improvement. Swimmers want to swim faster, high jumpers want to jump higher, weightlifters want to lift more weight. The goals dictate the method of practice. The bar is set. By exercising without goals, people became mere exercisers, rather than particular types of athletes. My clients couldn't hold onto tricep extension exercises or squats. I began to search for something sustainable that they could hold onto for life, something that would transcend quick fixes. A system like yoga, but something more complete that wouldn't need complementing with nutrition and resistance exercises, which are necessary to retain muscle mass and bone density. Something that would not confuse them about the role of food, which is not only supposed to nurture but to control body weight, or the role of exercise to increase strength and flexibility. This is why The Happy Body was created—as a holistic, long-term solution.

Many of our clients achieve THB and they love the feeling of well-being and the high level of fitness that goes along with it. Still, they may occasionally fall for a new fitness book or new exercise program, simply because everyone else is doing it. Once they exhaust all the quick fixes, however, they usually come back to THB. When they do, they all say the same thing: "I never felt better than I did when I followed The Happy Body program."

The resistance to embracing a new lifestyle is rooted deeply in our emotions. After years of living a certain way we develop strong personal habits. We are influenced by the culture we live in, and through exposure to the seductions of advertisements and media, we buy into projections of what they want us to buy or what our lifestyle should be. When deciding, it is the feelings that we have at the moment that will make the difference in our choice. That's why we devoted our lives to educate people so the intellect can influence and direct us in those emotional situations, allowing us to chose what we need in spite of what we want at that instant.

We all want a happy body, but the bigger the damage, the longer we wait to do something about it and the more drastic and desperate we become. The liposuction, the plastic surgeries, the drugs, the supplements, the special treatments in spas—the list goes on and on. The change is not earned legitimately but rather bought in as a quick-fix solution. We fall in love with the outside fixes offered by others. To change internally is to acquire new habits and ways of thinking and feeling. It is addictive to see quick changes in appearance, outside ourselves, without any real work—the same kind of work that is necessary for earning a degree or entering a profession. To really fall in love with something is a process, one that takes time. The process calls for overcoming difficulties and integrating new solutions into one's life. You cannot fall in love with quick fix weight loss, because it has to stop, and stopping means falling out of love.

When most of our clients come to us initially, they are depressed, even though they don't always realize it. They do not like what they have become and they are in search of how best to change. They are not aware of their state of mind at the time. Only perspective enables them to understand where they used to be and where they currently are. This perspective assures them that they are on the right path. They own their changes and are proud of themselves. They start to agree to adjustments they have to make because of age and lower metabolic rate, to control their weight. They start to agree to exercise, even though they never liked it, because their body deterio- rates. That's the only way to keep it strong and flexible, to maintain good posture, avoiding pains and surgeries.

Wandering off to look into something new is normal. This is a common transition, as we first have to lose something of value, in order to recognize it for its true worth and fully appreciate it.

Less is More—Really?

You've probably heard many times that "less is more." And after believing that it's true, you shared that kernel of wisdom with others. If you shared it with somebody who was obese and wanted to lose weight, they would probably agree with you, but if you shared this with somebody who treated anorexics, they would probably disagree. If you told it to a rich man who was tired of his lifestyle, he'd agree with you, but if you said the same thing to a poor man you could get into trouble. You probably would not like the idea of making less next month and would be happy if your boss gave you a raise. And you probably would not like the idea of getting obese and would be happy if you saw your weight drop on the scale. So the main question is really how much more or how much less in a particular situation.

You could say that in America we constantly think about more. More is a sign of progress and wealth—more money, more food, more health, more years to live. The idea of more keeps us motivated and constantly on task to make our dreams come true—a house, a spouse and then a family. Is there something wrong with this idea? I don't think so, so why do many people think that Americans are lost in more? It could be that while pursuing more in order to build a better life, we get addicted to that idea, and more spreads when less is needed. We eat and drink more than we need and we exercise more than we need. Life becomes hard to deal with. Instead of saving money, we spend more, and we experience needing more to just get by.

We lose our focus on the more that could create a better life for us and focus instead on the more that is not needed. For most of us, it just happens. We live our life and do not think critically about things like food or exercise. It does not occur to us that the triviality of food and exercise has anything to do with our failures. And normally it wouldn't, but we live in a free country and everyone has the right to more. If you were a cinnamon bun producer you would make as many buns as possible from the cheapest ingredients available and, most important, you would make these buns irresistible and crave-able so people would keep eating them and your business would thrive. Of course you could say "I would never do such a thing," but you would have to agree, then, that you might lose your business and go broke, and that is why you are not a food producer.

At first we think that we just need to work harder, and eight hours day becomes twelve. You get more money and everything seems fine. Of course the situation repeats itself after a while, and our day morphs to sixteen hours, six days a week. We spend four times more than we need to on food, more for gyms to exercise and more for diet pills and even more for surgeons. We live in a free market economy so we cannot expect the government to take care of us by telling business people what to do. So what is the solution to this more that makes us less?

You know that you cannot stop eating when you have enough, because the food is either too delicious or you enjoy yourself so much that you lose awareness of what is more. At this point you've lost touch with the American ideal that first built this country, the American who worked hard was decent and built a better future by never wasting his efforts. He was connected with the achievable dream and he reached for it even if it took his whole life, leaving the fulfillment of it for his children. So what is the solution?

It doesn't come from poor people who have never had abundance, because when they achieve it they usually have the same problem. Two years ago I visited Poland. I went to a popular lake with my high school friend and took in the scenery. While we were sitting and watching people pass by, Pawel asked, "Do see anything different?" I looked around and the only difference I saw was the many new buildings.

"I see that the surroundings have become a lot richer."

"Nothing else?" Pawel asked.

"No, nothing else," I said.

Pawel pointed to some kids and asked, "What about people, are they the same?"

I looked at the four boys: one tall and thin, two fatter than normal and one about 300 pounds. Behind them was a family. The man was about 400 pounds. It hit me then: I had never seen so many big people in Poland.

"They work hard and spend all the money on food. We have a small America here." Pawel said.

America is the first country in the world that reached abundance and is now in the process of learning to control it. Today we know that our government cannot help, neither can the food producers, so where is help to be found? It must come from within the individual. But how do we become people who know when less is appropriate or when more is necessary? To answer that question, we created The Happy Body, the program to help people to eat enough, exercise enough, and rest enough to live a waste-less life.

WHAT TO CUT

The woman sat looking down at the floor.
"Over and over I lose the fat and gain it back.
I feel that liposuction is my only solution."
The surgeon smiled gently.
"But what are we going to do with your brain?
Should we suck some of that out too?"
The woman was surprised.
"Why my brain?"
"Well, something makes you gain weight.
Nobody pours food into you."
The woman looked up.
"You know, you're a surgeon but you talk like a
philosopher.
Aren't you a surgeon anymore?"
"I am," the surgeon said.
"Day by day I remove fat from peoples' bodies
but it does not seem that there will be any end.
Some days I guess I just don't know where I should cut."

CHAPTER 11

Commitment

It was character that got us out of bed, commitment that moved us into action, and discipline that enabled us to follow through.

—Zig Ziglar

Our Lifestyle is Our Responsibility

Part One: Ignorance Is Death: How Diabetes Killed My Father

My father was diabetic, but he wasn't born with the condition. It was something that manifested in his late forties, progressing gradually until he had to inject himself with insulin. As a young girl, it was painful for me to watch him do this. I thought that he was just unlucky, that it was a matter of genetics. His mother had diabetes, so we accepted the idea that he had simply inherited this condition from her.

My older brothers often said that I looked exactly like my grandmother, so I was eager to meet her. I met her only once, since she lived on the other side of Poland and it was expensive for my family to visit her. I only saw her when she was hospitalized. What I saw lying in bed was a large, older woman, clearly in pain. She was very kind and friendly but somehow I was so frightened that I left the room, complaining that I had a headache and needed some fresh air.

I was definitely affected by the vision of what my future would be if I followed in my grandmother's or my father's footsteps. The only way they coped with this illness was through medicine. My family and I were actually thankful that we lived at a time when diabetics could get help and continue to function, working and taking care of their families. Although there was acceptance on my father's part, my mother tried to convince him to change his eating habits, which were obviously unhealthy. He would eat a lot of animal protein, such as fried pork chops, duck or chicken with skin, and hamburgers, along with potatoes, and very little vegetables or fruit.

My father was not in the habit of playing with his children, but I remember that he would sometimes spend uninterrupted time alone with me, which was very special. He would sit with me at a table with a cutting board in front of him, a loaf of bread and a chunk of lard, either smoked or covered with paprika. He would cut small squares of bread and top them with lard as I would talk with him about school, the books I was reading, or history, which was his favorite subject. Although I hated fat, I loved eating these small treats with him, not yet consciously understanding the power of habit, especially when driven by powerful emotions. My hunger for time with my father, having his undivided attention, was enough to overcome my aversion.

He made no effort to change his diet, and exercise never crossed his mind. My father followed the standards of the prevailing culture. He ate, worked, and slept for the purpose of resting up, so he would have enough energy to work. On most days, he worked at the bakery for 10-12 hours, sometimes Saturdays, too. His job was physically very demanding. I can only imagine now how depressed my father must have felt, and helpless, to see how his energy level was gradually diminishing, with longer recovery periods, leaving little time for other joys in life. And there was no one he trusted to tell him that his condition could be reversed or at least controlled with appropriate changes.

I remember one time my father suddenly started to scream from pain. He cried out that he was going to die. We all got really scared and my mother called the paramedics. That was a very uncharacteristic thing for my mother to do, making it clear that the situation was truly serious. The paramedics came with a doctor who examined my father and gave him some kind of medication, after which he fell asleep, for hours. When he woke up, he called my mother and asked her to make him pork chops with potatoes, because he was very hungry. She refused and got very upset with him for so quickly forgetting his pain and fear of dying. They argued with each other, with him telling her that she was trying to starve him by giving him the vegetable soup she had cooked while he was sleeping, and with her accusing him of being gluttonous and irresponsible. This incident later became a family joke after my father got better.

Still, my family didn't know much about diabetes before my father was diagnosed with this condition, or how to care for a person who had it. We children thought that adults knew about these things, and we trusted their ability to find solutions to these problems. My father's illness progressed slowly but steadily, from simply checking his blood sugar level, to injections. His quality of life suffered. I could always find him taking naps, several times a day, or drinking enormous amounts of liquids because he was constantly thirsty. But there was no talk about changing his lifestyle to improve the condition that he brought upon himself as a result of bad habits.

I emigrated from Poland before my father's health deteriorated drastically. He got an infection in his toe that developed into gangrene. His leg was amputated to the knee to prevent the spread, but he was not healing well and got progressively worse. He died six months after the surgery. He was 67 years old, and I was devastated. Out of the thousands of people that I've been able to help, I felt as if I had failed one of the closest people to me: my own father.

Only after many years of teaching did I understand that change has to come from within. People have to be inspired and motivated to generate that energy to make changes. That's one of the reasons we don't train people, but rather educate them. To get them to understand that they have choices, the only solution is to equip them with the tools they need to achieve a healthy and youthful lifestyle.

"You can lead a horse to water but you can't make him drink." I understand that I can share the knowledge and expertise that I have acquired over the years but it's up to others to make changes, on their own. Because once you are aware of things, there is no more deceiving yourself.

Lifestyle is critical to well-being, with diet and exercise playing a key role. As we age, we need to continuously adjust our diet and exercise, to stay in the best condition possible. I read this story many years ago, a story that made me rethink how I need to be to teach others about health and fitness. I needed to face my own challenges about food choices and exercises to find out what and how much is good for me. How much is enough to have a healthy and satisfying life.

Here is the story:

A mother brought her son to see a Master. She bowed to him with great respect and said,

"Master you are my last hope to help my son."

"What is the matter with your son?" he asked.

"I love my son, dearly, but he is addicted to sugar. He is diabetic and I fear he will lose his life soon. Would you please help him to stop eating sugar?"

The Master looked at the son with deep concern. Then he looked at the mother.

"Alright," he said. "Come back in one month." He stood up and left the room.

They came back a month later. The mother was very happy to see the Master, hopeful that he had found the solution for her son. The Master welcomed them, then said to the boy, looking straight into his eyes.

"Stop eating sugar. Now you can go."

There was deep silence for a moment, then he turned around to leave the room.

"That's it?" The mother's voice stopped the Master at the door.

"Yes," he answered.

"We had to wait the whole month to hear you say this?" The mother's voice sounded disappointed.

"Yes."

"Why?"

"Because a month ago I was eating sugar."

Part Two: Recipe for a Happier Life: Breaking Free from
Kitchen Bondage

As I was growing up, I observed how my mother's
life revolved around food and feeding our family. At
breakfast, she was already thinking about what to cook
for lunch. At lunch, she was making plans for dinner.
She was constantly engaged in meal planning, so that
there would be a variety of fulfilling, nutritious dishes to
make our family happy and healthy. Her challenge was
not only one of repertoire but also economy, as our family
was large and poor. Throughout the week, we ate what
we would now call vegetarian style soups, salads, pasta
and vegetable dishes. On weekends, we occasionally had
fish or meat. Every day we would eat things my mother
prepared from scratch. It was time consuming but it was
a lot cheaper then buying ready made products at local
stores, and homemade food was also superior to prepared
food in terms of taste and nutritional value.

My mother also planned for winter days when produce
was very expensive. So, seasonally, when there was an
abundance of fruit and vegetables and the prices on
those items would drop, we would buy large quantities
of whatever was cheapest. We pickled, canned and
made jars of preserves. Some vegetables (potatoes, beets,
carrots, turnips and celeriac, for example) could be stored
fresh in the basement, to get us through the winter
months.

This is how I learned from my mother the role of a
man and a woman in a marriage. The division of labor
was simple, dating back to the times of the cavemen. The

man brought the meat home and the woman cooked it. My father provided the money, while my mother bought and cooked the food.

When I got married, I ambitiously sought to correctly fulfill my duties as wife. Of course, food was one of the ways I wanted to please, nurture and entertain my husband. Besides what I learned at home from my mother, I would exchange recipes with my girlfriends, young wives themselves, and buy cookbooks, as well as clip new recipes from magazines. Although our lifestyle was different from that of our parents (we were both studying and working), I tried to maintain the high standards I had set for myself. After a while, all this gourmet cooking and laboring in the kitchen took its toll. I became tired and frustrated because time in the kitchen was siphoning off too much time from other things that were higher priorities.

Finally, one day at the dinner table, Jerzy looked at me and said, "I'm not going to eat this dinner. You look tired and unhappy, which makes it impossible to enjoy the beautiful meal you've prepared. I've been observing this for a while. I see how you spend so much time on studying cookbooks, shopping and standing in the kitchen for hours on end. When you finally sit down at the table, you are tired and irritable. After dinner, you are in the kitchen once again, cleaning and scrubbing pots and pans. If you are doing this for me, I would rather eat something simple, like a bowl of soup, and have you here with me, energetic and smiling. What's most important to me is the quality of the time we spend together."

I sat there silently. At first all kind of emotions were moving through me. I was angry because I prepared a delicious dinner, I guess, and expected appreciation for my efforts from my husband. Then I thought about how he watched me all this time not saying anything, but patiently waiting for me to get it on my own. Then it struck me: my husband doesn't expect or want me to be a kitchen slave like his mother or mine. Then I got really sad.

I started to think about my mother singing while she was doing laundry or washing the dishes, how her beautiful voice resounded throughout our home. Just like the Brazilian opera singer Bidu Sayao. I thought about her swollen, arthritic hands that, with just with a few quick sketches, produced magical images of lions, dolls, and trees with intricate branches. She could be very creative in designing and sewing clothes for the whole family, and in many other household arts, but she did all these things out of necessity. I believe she could have become a master of anything she chose to pursue, if only her life had been a little different. If she saw that she could chose to do things differently.

As I watched her as I was growing up, admiring all the wonderful skills she had, I also, deep down, feared ending up like her. I wanted to discover and follow my passion in life. Know what I could do and be good at. I wanted to live a happy, fulfilling life, without regrets.

I, along with many women, struggled, and many more to come will go through the same dilemma of how much time to spend in the kitchen preparing food to feed and nurture our families, not buying pre-prepared foods at the grocery store or expensive restaurant fare where there is no control over the quality or ingredients. That is why Jerzy and I simplified the idea of cooking. Our plan is easy: we make soups daily for lunch, which we love. Once a week we make our own batch of healthy food bars made out of dried fruit, nuts, seeds and dark chocolate. Every morning we start with our own prepared smoothie or green juice, and we use pulp for vegetable pate as a snack by adding lemon, ginger, garlic, avocado and fresh herbs. We also use fruit with nuts for snacks, among other choices. Our weekdays are simple; we focus on what we need to do workwise and spending quality time with our daughter. Weekends are more relaxed so we might occasionally go out for lunch or dinner to our favorite restaurant. We also like to entertain at home, and often enjoy cooking creatively and spending leisure time with friends. We found out that simple, good quality food is the best remedy to keep our bodies healthy in these fast paced, challenging times.

Strategy

Imagine a ship on the ocean. Without a rudder, and power to move, it would float wherever the wind and waves carried it. If you don't care where you go then this scenario would fit you, but if you do know where you want to go, then you need a plan for how to get there. But having a plan doesn't guarantee that you'll reach the goal. To reach your destination successfully you also need a strategy to accommodate any possible scenario that could arise. Think about the ship again. The captain knows where to go and designs a plan, but the journey is long and full of surprises so he prepares for any storm coming his way. His plan is adjusted accordingly to weather patterns and other unexpected situations like the illness of his workers, hijackers, or damages to the boat. In every moment he has to know whether to change course because of a storm, call for help in the case of a health crisis, or make repairs to the boat or head to port for assistance. If his strategy is right, he can save the boat or the lives of his crew. Consequently, he studies extensively beforehand so he is prepared to prevent any possible disaster.

Janine had one weakness while trying to lose weight. She traveled extensively for her work, spending hours in meetings that left her tired at the end of a day. After work, around 6pm, drinks were usually served and then dinner followed about one hour later. After two drinks she would get very hungry, so when dinner arrived she would eat far more than she had planned to. When

Janine returned home she was four pounds heavier and frustrated. She looked at me and said, "I know my goal and the plan, but as soon as I have my second drink, nothing matters anymore—I watch myself eating as if I hadn't eaten for days. I need a strategy."

I told her that a strategy always involves more than one option. I told her that the best way is to have some solutions prepared before your meeting is over. As soon as you decide which is best for the moment, it will be easier to stick to the plan. Here are some solutions:

1. Just after the meeting, go to your room and take a short nap. It will rejuvenate you and it will be easier to stick to your plan. Go back just before dinner starts. You will be refreshed and enjoy a drink and a moderate dinner.

2. Decide to have only one drink throughout the evening, sipping slowly. Add some water to your glass as soon as you drink some off. You will have enough alcohol in your body to keep you happy and relaxed, yet still sound intelligent. Then choose to eat only vegetables at dinner.

3. Have one or two drinks but don't touch food at all.

4. Don't have any drinks. Instead, have some water with lemon in a cocktail glass so you don't draw unwanted attention for not drinking.

5. Don't go out to dinner at all.

Strategy is essential for any kind of success. A chess player masters as many moves as possible. The player who remembers more options can easily predict the other player's plan and choose a strategy to trap the other player and win the match. If our goal is to control food intake and lose weight, we also need to predict all possible scenarios so we don't end up surprised, without a strategy. For example, in choice number two, you decided to have one drink and eat only vegetables, yet when you come to dinner you find out that there are no vegetables available. Now, if you have a strategic solution ready for this you can easily implement it and continue to follow your plan. You can decide to have a drink and go for a dinner somewhere else; or decide not to drink, talk for some time, and then go elsewhere for dinner; or decide to eat what is available but closely monitor the amount.

Every solution should be rehearsed until it becomes organic and is easy to implement when needed. Practice going out to dinner with friends and decide which option to follow. If you choose not to have a drink during dinner, then you should practice this method until you have complete control. At that point, you will see that you can enjoy the occasion whether you have a drink or not.

Our habits change slowly. If, for example, you weigh 170 and lose 40 pounds, your body is now 130 but your mind is still set at 170 and it will do everything to drag you back to where you were before. Your mind needs to experience many transitions to support a new, 130-pound body. These transitions are really changes in our beliefs. At the beginning of your journey, for instance, you might believe that you cannot control your weight because you travel. Something powerful enough has to happen to inspire you and motivate you to change your mind. We learned through twenty years of practice that stories are the most powerful tools for motivating people to change their beliefs. The right words spoken at the right time can help the mind's transformation truly take hold.

LIFE'S PLAN

I will be forty tomorrow
and I feel as if gravity
becomes stronger every year.
Life at forty does not plan
to make you better.
Its plan is to make you worse.
That's very depressing.
I thought you knew that
depression is included with aging.
Let's not talk about it.
It gives me chills.
Then, I need to ask you one question:
Which is better,
to wait for an accident
or to prevent it?
Prevention takes energy.
So does an accident.

CHAPTER 12

Fulfillment

The chief condition on which, life, health and vigor depend on, is action. It is by action that an organism develops its faculties, increases its energy, and attains the fulfillment of its destiny.

—Colin Powell

A Mindset or Rather, a Mindstyle?

Over the years, we've coached, trained and mentored many people who have come to us with body issues. They hope to heal physical injuries, alleviate chronic pain or improve body image.

The condition of our bodies can tell us what is out of balance in our lives, as well as how we arrived there. We tend to overdo, or not do enough. To discover what is out of balance with each individual, we embark on a journey of exploration. After that, we set out to find solutions that will result in a happy body—and within that body, a happy mind and spirit to safeguard it.

What you do now will matter in a week, a month or a year. There is a certain cumulative effect that enables us to achieve the desired results for you in the future. In working with people of different backgrounds, educational levels, financial status, genetic make-up and physical characteristics, we have identified a certain mindstyle that manifests itself physically. To me 'mindset' seems a rigid word. I choose instead to use 'mindstyle' because of our evolving choices. It's a 24-hour practice. In fashion, style means something: how we dress, furnish our house, pick a piece of jewelry, etc. The sum of all our choices creates a certain ambiance that is our lifestyle. The same goes for our choices about food, exercise and deciding how to relax. Choices. That is what distinguishes us from others, and make us an individual.

Even though our clients come from different walks of life, people with this mindstyle have one thing in common: the constant pursuit of improvement. In this quest, they are true achievers, constantly seeking ways to better themselves.

Our client list includes many psychologists, who often ask about the success rate for The Happy Body Program and whether there are particular groups of people that have more success than others. After some thought and investigation, we discovered that there is a particularly high success rate among athletes and businesspeople. Their success seems to be tied to high levels of motivation.

Another group with a high success rate are those who work one-on-one with others to seek results for those individuals: coaches, mentors, therapists and others. Because they are responsible for the success of other people, they are often put into situations that force them to achieve. They have to "walk the talk." Professional rank, however, does not predict success.

People with particular characteristics tend to succeed, regardless of profession. They are well-grounded people, who are not intimidated by long-range thinking. For such individuals, every day counts and every training session counts, as does every meal and every conversation. They see every day as a continuation of the previous one, creating a new day that is better than the last. This person assumes beforehand that two to five years are needed to create a new lifestyle. On some level, he or she is aware—perhaps not completely consciously, but at some level¬—that it takes time. Eventually, after a year or more, the individual achieves at least a certain level of mastery of the skills in question.

What we have also found is that there are three types of people that approach The Happy Body. The first involves those who are very excited and want to do more than they are asked: "the athletic mind". They are driven to achieve, without the need for additional external motivation. They tend to overdo things and spin out of control. They need guidance and coaching in order to actually achieve their goals.

The second type is the opposite of that: "the wishful mind". These are the people who need to be constantly inspired and motivated to do things. While the first type does too much, the second type does too little. In our experience, they are motivated by seeing other people in their environment who are changing and relaying their stories. These clients transform through the experience of the story, emerging with new perspective and energy. Maybe for a day or two, they will be inspired. Then another story has to be told, to inspire them anew. The process continues, until the person becomes transformed into the third type—"the Olympian mindstyle".

This third group of people who embrace The Happy Body Program consists of individuals who fall between the first two groups. They are ready, emotionally and mentally. They only need a short period of coaching to become independent. When they get it, they want to go home and just do it. Achieving what we strive for, or plan for, requires mastering a healthy balance between not enough and too much.

Although many people who come to see us are well educated, they are nonetheless emotional, making daily decisions based on their feelings. When people are masters of something, it doesn't mean they are masters of all.

Let's take a fictitious client we'll call "Julia." Julia struggled for a long time to change her personal habits and behavior. She was an accomplished psychologist, with multiple advanced degrees, who was writing a book. As an outlet for stress, she would frequently play solitary card games on the computer, often for hours on end.

But in the morning, she wouldn't have enough energy to do the exercises. She would then overeat because she thought more food would give her more energy. As a member of "the wishful mind" category, she needed ongoing motivation.

As for you, the reader, to achieve the best results with the program, you need to start by figuring out which of the three categories describes you. This will tell you which approach you need to follow. Do you need to be slowed down or do you need to be empowered to go forward?

The choices we make in the present moment determine who we become. So if a lifestyle is an adapted way of living, then whatever contributes to who we become is not something solid and unchangeable but a malleable entity. The moment that we decide to change certain things about ourselves that don't work anymore, we set ourselves on a journey toward positive change.

Let's start with an exploration of what it is that you want to happen. What would be your motivation to change? Is it based on desire (for something you want) or fear (of something you don't want)?

Pause at this point to consider your personal motivations, and write them down.

Here are two examples, offered by our clients:

"I am getting older and I would love to be able to enjoy my life as someone who is physically active, mentally sound, spiritually aware and connected with others."

This illustrates motivation based on desire.

And:

"I am getting older and I fear aging the way my mother did, becoming stiff, overweight, in pain, mentally deteriorated and lacking spiritual purpose."

This illustrates motivation based on fear.

The change can only happen when you are engaged in doing something that is challenging. This is what we call crossing borders.

If you want to change, you need to emigrate to a new place (which can be a state of mind or a level of involvement, rather than a physical location). Think of emigrating to The Happy Body as your passport to success in life.

The process of emigration involves five key steps:

1. Realize that there is something essential that doesn't work for you anymore. This should prompt you to ask: What is it that doesn't work for me?

2. Make your best attempt to change whatever it is that does not work for you. Ask yourself: What have I done to effect a change?

3. Come to terms with the reality that there is something fundamentally beyond your control that you cannot change. Rather than submitting to the controlling force, you make the decision to remove yourself from the situation.

4.   Decide on a plan for building a better future. Here you let your imagination run free, formulating appealing options and then selecting the one you regard as the most desirable.

5.   Execute your plan. The best plan is only valuable if it is actually carried out.

Jerzy and I are first-generation immigrants from Poland. We escaped in 1985, when it was still a communist country under Russian domination. At the time there were no indications of any foreseeable changes, making us feel trapped and hopeless about our future and the future of our country. We were young and ready to create our own life, though not a life that would have been predictable. We had arrived at a crossroad and realized that the only way to save ourselves was to leave Poland. Leaving involved the possibility of never being able to come back or see our families or friends again.

One day we were sitting in a line of cars waiting to cross the border from Poland into Germany. The line was so long that we were not able to see the booths up ahead where the customs officials were waiting. Drivers and passengers were stuck, resigned, in their vehicles.

Some were truck drivers, sitting alone in the cabs of their large trucks. Others were families in old, beaten-up cars. Most were returning from shopping trips, bringing black market goods to sell to supplement their incomes. There were also young men and women dressed in business attire, driving luxury vehicles. We were all sharing the same moment, regardless of where we were coming from. We were all crossing borders.

Not long after we arrived in the United States, the Berlin wall came down, followed by all the changes in Eastern Europe. Our first visit to Poland was in 1989. Sitting in the car, lined up at the border, I was looking through the window at the Polish people, my people, and thought about Jerzy and me, how different we had become since we emigrated. "Crossing borders," both physically and mentally, we had gained a new perspective on life. What formerly hadn't seemed possible, or even imaginable, became something that was in our power to determine.

The experiences we had been through, the challenges that we had overcome, during a short span of four years, had transformed us into different people. The changes had occurred on many levels: like a stone dropped in a pond, it rippled outward, profoundly affecting all areas of our lives.

From comfort to discomfort, to stability that made us comfortable, and then into a state of discomfort again: that was the pattern we were following. That was our road to change. There were certain principles that we applied, whether it was in developing our business, our education, or our personal growth, which all manifested what we wanted in life.

After a while, we started to see the similarity between going through the process of emigration and going through the process of achieving fitness, weight loss or health: You want to transform yourself into someone different. Different means new and unfamiliar, which is inherently unsettling. To assimilate into a new culture and be happy, you must accept that new culture and everything that comes with it, including a new lifestyle.

"Culture shock" is usually a stage in this process. Another aspect relates to the friends and family members you leave behind. Whether you are aware of them or not, the emotional attachments and habits you formed over a period of many years are powerful; you will feel homesick, a longing for your old lifestyle and you'll experience a frustrating desire to return to the past. With time, you become comfortable in a new culture and eventually even learn a new language in which you can express yourself and think. (Thinking in a new language is not usually considered, but it happens over time.)

This naturally calls for a lot of effort, a lot of work. How many people come to a new country but don't learn the language? There are certainly many who simply blend into their own small ethnic enclaves, where they can survive by speaking their old languages and following old habits.

The feeling of being suspended between two cultures often interferes with making the smooth transition from the point of origin to the new environment. You must make peace with the decision to leave the old behind before you can successfully embrace the new, although you can always return to the old, if only for the purpose of borrowing elements to integrate into your new life.

The process of change is similar to the process of mourning, because by the end, the person we used to be will no longer exist. We will become someone else, someone new.

Once we understand that we need to change, we will be in denial if we avoid the work ahead of us. It's easy to tell ourselves that we're doing just fine with our halfway attempts; we might even isolate ourselves to avoid facing the approaching change. We might start feeling resentment, privation or the anger that results in feelings of persecution and rage over life not being fair. Next comes the bargaining or attempts at manipulation, which, at the end of the day only delays in what needs to happen. Once we realize that we cannot do things the old way and, at the same time, become someone new, depression sets in. Depression causes stagnation, and the road to becoming a new self becomes more difficult and requires outside help.

When we accept what we need to do, we will start moving forward, and start seeing small increments of change grow into recognizable results, based on new practices. And that is the beginning of change. Whatever changes we achieve, the process is similar to thinking about getting rich. People don't even want to make the effort to become rich, because they might fail and lose what little they already have. Even worse, they might make fools of themselves. For many, the decision-making and labor that is required stifle the desire to even try. Once we stop struggling and accept what we need to do in order to become what we want to become, the real work begins and the results will be quickly visible—that's what makes us feel proud, fulfilled, and happy.

As we start on the journey of becoming a fuller, more expansive person, we will have to work against the influence of many things: personal habits, family traditions, and the education, customs, and culture assimilated from our communities. Over time, we will go through all kinds of experiences, adaptations and adjustments, which are necessary to shape a new self. We need to shed an old skin and grow another. The new changes need to become second nature for us. That is why all the diets and programs that focus on fixing the "problem" don't bring the desired results. When the illusion of fixing stops, the real work begins.

The part of the mind that is intelligent is based on words, on language. The emotional part of our mind chooses, and that part doesn't have language. Most of us are making decisions based on primal feelings, not the intellect. As if our survival depends on it, what is emotional wants to dominate. To change, you need tools, a manual to follow, and a commitment to consistent practice, to ensure the results you want.

Anything that is new will bring frustration. Life is a constant frustration. If we give in to frustration, we will not do what needs to be done and will be frustrated afterwards from not getting the desired results. The frustration builds because we keep doing the same thing over and over. We keep repeating the same mistakes. We get poor results, which creates dissatisfaction and depression. In our minds, we create the idea that what we wanted at the beginning of the journey is no longer needed. This belief takes us back to where we started. It creates enough force to make us abandon the practice, abandon pursuing what was desired in the first place. The aspiration itself becomes a burden. Then we get depressed. Over and over, we repeat the same destructive process.

But some of us are able to tolerate frustration, the difficulties connected with learning new skills. As time passes, we get closer to our goal, which makes us happier and motivates us to keep going until we achieve it.

So before you begin, you must examine your intellectual and emotional state of mind, because the change is not going to come from feelings—you might get stuck there—but from imagination, and that has to be developed. For that you need someone to guide you. We need directions and new habits. It's easy to see in children how, if they are not helped at a certain time, we fail them as parents. We need to help our children establish patterns, to complete homework and be on time for school, to achieve high grades and a certain level of education. If not, our children will fall behind and get so frustrated that they slowly fail.

With a constant pursuit of small incremental improvements, the new experience will eventually change your feelings. The visualization of what you want will push you forward. If we focus on what we can we change, then we gain control over our body in some way and we can move on.

Some things that we can't change include:
- Height
- Gender
- Color of eyes
- Hereditary disabilities

Some things that we can change are:
- Physical and intellectual activities
- Muscle size through training
- Hormone levels through physical activity

- Eating habits, to change body composition
- Amount of food to affect body weight
- Frequency of eating to regulate insulin

Since the body is physical, we can change it through physical activity and the food we eat. We need to keep in mind what we want to achieve from exercise. Most people have general ideas what they want to see happen through exercise and, when asked, will tell you something general like "they want to be healthy or fit."

On the other hand, if you ask an athlete, either they or their coach will know exactly what results they need to achieve. Any sport has goals. When it comes to fitness, those goals initially look vague: losing weight, getting stronger and getting healthier.

So what does it say about us when we engage in an activity without knowing what to do and where we're supposed to arrive, once we embark on the journey?

Our daughter Natalie has been pursuing gymnastics for several years. She loves it and tells us that she cannot imagine her life without it. The demand of pursuing her passion also falls on us as parents in making time to drive her, fund her, because it requires her being in the gym and practicing at least twenty hours per week.

Between her schoolwork and gymnastics there is little time left for anything else. In gymnastics there are over five million young people just in the USA laboring hours and hours per week for years, but only five will go to the Olympics. Does this mean that if you are not one of these girls who are among the top gymnasts that you should quit now?

This is where I would like to draw a parallel — suppose that you are older, say in your fifties or sixties or even seventies? Should you just resign yourself to a state of decline and give up the fight for a better way of being? Even if you are not going to become an Olympian, there are other benefits from pursuing any discipline. You will challenge yourself in many ways to become a better person. You will overcome many difficulties and learn how to be graceful in winning or losing. Try to find solutions if you encounter problems among new challenges. What matters at the end of the day is that you will be better than before you started, in spite of the passing time.

Fighter vs. Warrior

A warrior in life is a quiet person. He knows that war is long and takes a lot of energy and preparation, so he does not react to those who provoke a fight unless he is ready for a war. A fighter, on the other hand, is always ready for any fight. He can easily snap on a freeway, at the dinner table, or during a business meeting. He usually pays a high price for his reactive personality. He can cause an accident or lose a family or business, all thanks to his high temper. But he cannot help himself: As soon as the possibility of conflict appears, his adrenaline is high and he is ready for any action, even though it could be fatal. By that time he no longer has any awareness of future consequences.

When Josh came I was still with a new client who needed help understanding the food plan, so I had to spend more time with him before he left. I showed Josh a place on a couch and asked him if he would like some tea.

"No, I'm full," he said, so I told him I would be back in a moment. When I returned after seven minutes and sat down opposite him, he snapped. "What kind of business is this? I waited here for seven minutes and nobody came. I hope I won't pay for these minutes! You completely disrespected me." Josh was shaking from anger so I said I'm sorry, but I had a client who was eighty years old and had difficulty understanding my directions. Josh shot right back, "Then you should have somebody else here to help me so I don't pay for sitting!"

At this point I thought it would be better if Josh went home, so I said so and told him that I didn't think I would be able to help him. Josh shot back that he didn't want to go home. It was a strange response, and I was not sure if Josh had really understood me so I said it again: I think you should go home. Josh shot back, again, "I don't want to go home." It puzzled me, so I said, "Why don't you want to go home? You definitely don't like this place. You don't like the way we treated you and probably everything else here." Josh looked at me and said, "I have pains I cannot stop."

"Pains?" I said. "Where"? Josh began talking to me about his elbows. His forearms were less developed than his upper arms. It was obvious to me that his forearms could not carry over the power that was coming from his upper arms, and therefore could not recover from the physical stress. He had a sort of "tennis elbow." The only way to heal the elbows and prevent the pain from returning in the future was to make the elbows stronger than the arms. Josh continued with his story: "I have these pains in my elbows that just don't go away. Over the years I've had two surgeries, I've taken painkillers and have had adjustments, I've been treated by a physical therapist but the pain remains. I don't know what else to do. Somebody told me about you, so I came here. That's why I don't what to go home." When Josh talked about his elbows, I saw how the expression on his face changed from anger to the frustration and vulnerability of a person who needs help. As soon as I saw his pain, I shifted from a fighter to a warrior in my response. "We can heal this, but it will take us about a year or two. Our goal is to heal your elbows and the only way to achieve that is to make them stronger."

Josh was doubtful. "Well, I tried to do it by myself and with trainers and as soon as I begin any type of training, the pain became worse."

I knew that Josh's problem was treatable, so I laid out my strategy for him. "We have to be very subtle and patient," I said. "Our goal is clear, now we need to design a plan to achieve it. First, we have to find exercises and weight that your elbows will be able to tolerate without getting worse, then we will increase the weight and watch the pain. If the pain is the same and we lift more weight then we're on the right track. As months pass, you'll notice that sometimes the pain is less. Then you'll have a day or two without pain. And after that you'll have three or four days without pain, and finally one day you'll notice that you don't have any pain at all. At this point the pain is just under your threshold, but the problem is still there. We will continue to work on getting stronger and taking that pain farther and farther from your threshold, until the problem is eliminated. When the pain is deep enough you'll forget about it; I expect this will happen in about two years. Are you ready for your journey?"

"I was always ready," Josh responded. I smiled. "Let's begin."

Three months later, Josh noticed that his pain had lessened slightly. His respect and trust returned; he didn't look at his watch anymore. All he wanted to do was whatever came next to contribute to the plan. He no longer cared that he spent a full hour with me and paid for it. Sometimes he came and spent only ten minutes before he was ready to go. Yet he still paid for sixty minutes. Time on the clock didn't bother him anymore. One day I said, "Josh, the first day that you came, you debated every dollar that you spent, and today you're paying for sixty minutes but you're using only ten. Tell me how this change happened." Josh smiled and said, "Let me tell you a story...."

One time, there was a ship owner who had a problem with an old boiler. Whatever he did, he couldn't make it work. Finally, he called in a plumber to fix it. The plumber came, looked over the boiler for a moment, listened to it, and gave it a kick. Instantly, the boiler started to work properly. The ship owner thanked the plumber and asked him for his bill.

"A thousand dollars," said the plumber.

"A thousand dollars for kicking the boiler!"

"No," the plumber said. "One dollar for kicking the boiler. Nine hundred and ninety-nine dollars for knowing where and how to kick the boiler."

Josh concluded, "I understand that I pay for knowledge, and the less time I spend the better for me, even if it's only ten minutes. I don't want to spend sixty minutes with someone else and still not know what to do."

Josh had shifted from a fighter to a warrior. As soon as he connected to his problem and decided to fix it, the understanding helped him accept what efforts and time would be necessary. He stopped fighting small fights, like being angry that he was not respected, and focused on the war, which required a plan, strategies and a long-term commitment.

The Happy Body is a plan for a warrior, not a fighter. It declares war against aging by applying the wisdom of how to deal with such a powerful force. It educates us and helps us to strategize a plan of action to age slowly, so we can adapt to passing time and rejoice that we don't feel the age we are. In this way we can be proud that we are old warriors, instead of hiding our age like fighters.

I KNOW WHAT I WANT

After Daniel tasted one apple
he would eat until all the apples were gone.
When his wife came home, Daniel
had finished his eleventh apple,
the last one from the basket.
You'll never stop being diabetic
if you eat so many apples, Joan said.
I'm used to being sick.
What about wasting money?
You don't care about that, either?
No. I love apples.
But you ate eleven of them,
one would be enough.
She took Daniel's hand
and walked with him to the bathroom.
Then she pulled out a hundred-dollar bill,
threw it into the toilet and flushed it down.
Have you lost your mind? Daniel screamed.
That's a ten-day supply of apples.
I'd rather see that in the toilet,
than all those apples inside of you.
Then she left the bathroom.
Daniel still watched, as water filled the toilet.
He came to the living room and sat in his armchair.
It had been ten years since he was diagnosed.
He looked at the table and chairs,
simple but clean and strong.
Then he noticed his wife.
She was sitting in the corner drinking tea

and watching birds eating seeds.
She was neither upset nor irritated.
He didn't notice how quiet she had become.

ABOUT THE AUTHORS

Aniela and Jerzy Gregorek came to the United States from Poland in 1986 as political refugees during the Solidarity Movement. Elite professional weightlifters, they have both won multiple world championships and set world records. While working as trainers in L.A., they became aware that people needed a dramatic change in lifestyle, not simply an hour a day of supervised exercise, to achieve real results. The Happy Body Program grew from this insight, supplying definable goals and a plan to sustain improvement. By coaching the UCLA weightlifting team and observing trained athletes they began to integrate scientific principles to better refine and expand their system.

Today The Happy Body Program has helped thousands of people transform their bodies and lives. In working with clients over thirty years, Aniela and Jerzy discovered the power of stories to help change belief systems and habits. It was by addressing feelings, not simply absorbing information, that clients were able to implement the simple but often difficult solutions they faced with diet and exercise. At this point Aniela and Jerzy realized that their own experiences with immigration, art and poetry gave them a different perspective, one that could make a tremendous difference. They knew that even informed clients were still vulnerable to making the wrong choices. It takes emotional intelligence, built up through a different kind of support that addresses the unconscious side of ourselves, before a client can be able to really feel "I got this."

In 1998 Jerzy and Aniela earned MFAs in writing from the Vermont College of Fine Arts. Their poems and translations have appeared in numerous publications, including The American Poetry Review. Jerzy's poem "Family Tree" was the winner of Amelia magazine's Charles William Duke Longpoem Award in 1998. In 2002, the National Endowment for the Arts awarded him a literature fellowship to support the translation from Polish into English of selected poems by Maurycy Szymel. This culminated in the publication in 2013 of *The Shy Hand of a Jew* by Cross-Cultural Communications, which the following year published a collection of Jerzy's own poetry, entitled *Sacred and Scared*.

As Aniela and Jerzy engaged in writing their own poetry, translating the poetry of others and deepening their understanding of world events and human suffering, they began to build a bridge between science and art, intelligence and emotion. They introduced a selection of classical music and floral images for relaxation, *The Happy Body Ambience*, a book of poems called *Food for Your Soul*, three books of Platonic dialogues, *The Master/ Fatalist* series, to address the invisible emotional dimension that other programs ignore. Compiled from decades of experience, *I Got This* is the latest contribution to this work, offering the right words to the right person at the right time.

Aniela and Jerzy live with their daughter Natalie and a variety of pets in Woodside, California.